Search For Serenity

by
LEWIS F. PRESNALL

Published by

U. A. F.

2880 South Main

Suite 210

Salt Lake City, Utah 84115

i

CONTENTS

FOREWORD

Some people meet life with zest; others seem to live in a state of chronic dissatisfaction. Two people, confronted with identical problems, often react in entirely different ways. One will make the best of the immediate situation. He will find some seeds for enjoyment in the most difficult circumstance. The other individual may lapse into a state of misery.

Those who are perpetually miserable, unhappy and bored with life do not need to remain that way. There may be little they can do at the moment to change their circumstances, but there is a great deal which they could do about their own reactions. As a very realistic friend once said to me, "Misery is optional." Misery is inside one's self. It is part of one's own feelings. We can all change the way we feel about things or people or circumstances.

This book is about people who have found it necessary to change the way they feel. They have learned that one's feelings are largely the result of certain complex patterns of habit. To change these emotional habits requires understanding, patience and self-discipline. In simple language this book attempts to describe some of the practical ways in which one can replace misery with serenity.

There are many friends whose helpful ideas have gone into these pages. I would especially like to thank them. They have contributed to the common fund of practical knowledge without which emotional growth could only come by hard personal experience. Also, I would like to thank the two individuals who shared in the transcription of notes and the typing. They gave a great deal beyond this routine work by adding their helpful criticism of style and content. They are only nameless here because they prefer it that way.

I am indebted to Alfred A. Knopf, Inc. for permission to use excerpts from Kahlil Gibran's book, "The Prophet"; to Simon and Schuster, Inc. for material borrowed from David H. Fink's "Release From Nervous Tension," and to Dr. Alfred E. James, Assistant Chief Surgeon, Chino Mines Division, Kennecott Copper Corporation, for reviewing and making suggestions in connection with Chapter II. I also owe much in the way of appreciation to Clyde W. Gooderham, to the organization which he represents and to his wife, Marie, for their encouragement and faith in the project.

There are several other quotations and references for which I have given appropriate credit within the text whenever the author's name is known.

Lewis F. Presnall

February 20, 1958.

Chapter I

The Search for Serenity

No one can learn to be at home in his own heaven until he has learned to be at home in his own hell.

The full appreciation of inner serenity is achieved only by those who have been forced to face their own weaknesses, their own limitations and the possibility of their own inner failures.

The bed rock of enduring serenity is found at the point where one realizes his own limitations—that point where one finds it necessary to choose between life and death; between the will to live and the surrender to hopelessness. He must then decide whether to continue along the road to ego-centric self-sufficiency—and die; or whether he will make an effort to achieve self-understanding—and live.

Life deals more rigorously with some than others. There are a few fortunate people who will go through life without ever facing any crisis severe enough to make necessary such a radical choice. Because life has dealt with them rather gently, they will perhaps imagine they are stronger than those who have been pushed to the border-zone of sanity. Until a major crisis upsets the applecart of their lives, such people may feel a certain superiority to those whose collapse has led them to the mental clinic, the alcoholic treatment center or to consultation with a psychiatrist. They may smugly say to themselves, "It can't happen to me."

They are usually unaware that they daily display many symptoms of immaturity. They do not clearly see the dif-

1

ference between conduct which is adult and conduct which is emotionally childish. On the other hand, to those of us who have groped our way to the light out of the shadowy terror of our exaggerated fears, these distinctions between the mature and the immature are excessively clear. We can perceive them in ourselves and we recognize them in our acquaintances.

A startling example of this awareness occurred one evening in the men's ward of a mental hospital where I was trying, along with about twenty-five other patients, to put the pieces of my own inner mind back together.

One of our number was a tall, slender chap about twenty-seven years old. He was one of those solitary, timid individuals who had apparently never learned to be at home with other people. In the hospital, most of his waking hours were spent in washing his hands. When he got tired of washing his hands he scrubbed all the lavatories. During the evening he would take a chair by himself in the big ward room, where the rest of us would be reading, working jigsaw puzzles, or passing the time in conversation. We would always speak to him, but he was usually too withdrawn for conversation beyond a few occasional words.

After five or ten minutes in his chair, this chap would get up quickly, walk with determination to the washroom, and begin another round of hand scrubbing—just as though he had not already done the same thing fifty times that day.

We indulged him in his compulsion. We made a point never to be rude or to give him the impression that we thought his behavior peculiar. For, truly, we each knew that we were all just as sadly peculiar in our own ways.

But one evening this young man came into our group during the middle of an animated conversation among four other inmates, who were playing cards around a table. Apparently, he imagined the group was talking about him and making fun of him. Suddenly, without warning, he was a towering storm of fury. His face contorted with anger as he lashed out in a stream of profanity. We thought for a moment that he would undertake to thrash the whole crew

2

of us. As his tantrum progressed, he began to shake. Then he burst into tears and rushed back to his room.

Two of the men then got calmly to their feet, followed him to his room and spent over an hour talking quietly to the disturbed patient. They assured him that we all liked him, that no one was discussing him behind his back, nor held a grudge over what had happened. The skill and patience with which they did this would have done credit to the most understanding parent or older friend. Yet, they themselves were patients whose behavior had been so irrational that they were locked in the hospital by court order.

Had such an incident occurred anywhere except in a mental hospital, or among men with deep understanding of each other, a fight would have been inevitable. But these men had been trained by their own experiences to recognize the difference between adult behavior and an outburst of emotional immaturity.

The search for serenity begins with a willingness to discover and honestly recognize the areas in our own lives where we did not quite grow up.

All of us are inclined to make alibis for our resentments, our unreasonable angers, our fears and our particular prejudices. When we become angry and make fools of ourselves, we ask the audience of our friends, "Well, wouldn't you be mad, too?" When we become unreasonably suspicious we make an alibi by saying, "Experience has taught me that people are not to be trusted." When our fears prevent us from being generous we excuse ourselves by the common remark, "I have to take care of myself, no one else will."

Excuses! Alibis! Protective walls behind which we hide our own inner inadequacies!

The shock of crisis reveals to us just how feeble is this false-front of excuses. We think of crisis in terms of such events as the sudden death of a loved person, the pressure of a long or disabling illness, the loss of financial security. Sudden tragedy does, in many cases, produce an inner crisis. But this is not always true. If it were, then everyone faced by such events would suffer a nervous breakdown. Adversity only results in an inner crisis when it

3

comes in a form that threatens one's own special kind of emotional immaturity.

A strong wind is no threat to a vigorous lone tree growing on the prairie—one whose root system has pushed deep into the soil during many a summer storm. But go to a grove of giant fir in the Oregon forest, where the great trees have supported each other in their closeness for centuries. Eliminate all the trees in that grove except one, leaving that one exposed alone to the elements. Then wait until some howling winter night when a storm is raging. This tree has sturdily weathered dozens of such tempests in the company of his strong neighbor trees, but now it is unprotected. Unprepared by normal growth to withstand such wind pressure alone, this tree will crash thunderously to the ground.

Do not call a man a weakling because he falls. If he had known beforehand that he had a weakness, he would have taken precautions to strengthen himself for the storm ahead. As Kahlil Gibran so aptly pointed out, one should be thankful for the man ahead of him who stumbles, for in his stumbling those of us who follow are warned of the loose flagstone in life's stair which we all must climb.

When we observe the fall of some friend whom we have considered strong, we must remember that each man's weakness is only a little-boy quality which failed to complete its growth.

The tragedy of childish emotions lies in the fact that they are so easily hidden. An arm which stops growing at the age of five is quite obvious at the age of seven. It will be a serious handicap at the age of eighteen. Every effort will be made to discover the cause of such arrested growth and correct the condition. But a fear of the dark developed at the age of five can be carried into adult life hidden from one's friends and hardly admitted to oneself. Or the temper tantrums of a three-year-old can be continued into adulthood under the guise of "righteous indignation." We all know individuals who boast of their terrible tempers as though they thought it were admirable to display the undeveloped "limbs" of a childish emotion.

Attempting to meet the pressures of adult responsibilities with such immature equipment can only result sooner or later in a crisis.

What happens when crisis comes? Life is only saying to us, "Grow up or die." Faced with this threat to survival, millions try to ease the pain of living with a pill. Millions more find temporary escape through liquor. Others leave the realm of reality altogether or come apart at the seams in what is politely known as a nervous breakdown.

Crisis brings to such people a choice: emotional growth and survival, or continued stagnation and eventual death.

This is the place of torment and decision, for no person likes to admit that he is inadequate, especially if he has thought of himself as a success. The successful person likes to believe that he is successful because he is strong. As Frank M. Colby pointed out in one of his essays, in our topsy-turvy world it is quite often the lopsided man who "runs the fastest along the little sidehills of success."

As long as we continue in a series of unbroken successes we are not apt to obtain the humility necessary to recognize our own conspicuous immaturities.

In all fairness, it must be said that circumstances have favored many people with the kind of growth which leaves behind no trailing remnants of childhood emotions serious enough to hamper their adult activity. These are the fortunate ones. Growth ought to be this way for everyone. Unfortunately, this is not the case for so many of us.

Those of us who have been made to search for our serenity, in the wreckage of fear, guilt, self-pity, suspicion and resentment have found there are six steps on our road to recovery.

1. Admission of a need
2. A decision to let our lives be guided by the main stream of the universe
3. An honest search for self-understanding
4. A willingness to accept the help of others
5. Our utmost effort to join the human race
6. The development of new emotional habit patterns

to fit our newly-found insights about ourselves, about other people and about our world

There are a great many books which are helpful in giving suggestions for the first four steps. But steps five and six outline an important area of re-building one's life which has been largely neglected in books now available. It is in this area that so many people lose their way, even after a promising start toward happiness, peace of mind and adequate living.

There is a growing fraternity in the world today. It is the fraternity of those whose present successes have been built upon the wreckage of past failure. People who belong to this fraternity, which exists without a formal organization, have a common bond of experience. They help one another. They help others who come to them in trouble, seeking the strength and guidance which comes only with experience. This fraternity is made up of people who have known the locked doors of mental institutions. Among them are those to whom the seamy side of life is no strange garment. The language of the clinical institution, the jail, the penitentiary, are well known to members of this fraternity. Among them are some of our most respected citizens.

As a group, members of this fraternity are perhaps the most sane individuals in our society today. They know how to give. They know how to love their fellow men. They understand their own weaknesses and are tolerant of weakness in others. They are at home in the heaven of their newly-found serenity because they once learned in all honesty to face the inner hell of their own confusion.

When such people converse about their common experiences, they often mention the name of this one or that one who made a promising start toward recovery, only to suffer a tragic relapse.

There are many causes for such relapses, which often seem to occur in cases where the individual has had the best of help and made an excellent beginning. One of the most common difficulties, however, seems to be the prob-

6

lem of building the complex new habit patterns so necessary to emotional growth.

This is a life-time job for anyone who must search for his serenity. There are so many ways in which old habit patterns can reassert themselves. Recovered alcoholics call this a return to "stinking thinking" or the "dry drunk."

One who has been accustomed for years to harboring resentments finds it difficult to avoid dropping back into the old pattern of taking a small grievance and developing it into a fine, monumental, long-term resentment.

An individual who has been a practicing "worrier" all his life finds it easy to imagine some small future problem, fertilize it with liberal quantities of insomnia, water it with childhood fears and watch it develop into a colossal anxiety.

The same sort of thing can be done easily with such emotions as self-pity, guilt, sexual conflicts and jeolousy. For any of us who have suffered from extensive emotional immaturities, it is easy to retrace the patterns of the past. The ruts of old habits are worn deep.

It is always easier to drop one's wheels into the well-worn ruts of the past than to manage the careful steering necessary to ride the ridges.

The trick of cutting a new trail across life's muddy landscape can be a most difficult procedure.

This book is written for those of us who got stuck in the mud. We sat there spinning our wheels until the undercarriage was imbedded in mud and the wheels were in up to the axles. Then some kind person came along with a tow-chain, helped us jack up the wheels, threw some fence posts under the tires and got us running again.

Now all we need to know is how to steer this thing so it won't slide down into the fatal ruts again.

We had better learn and learn quickly. Perhaps next time we slip there will be no one available to give us the lift we need.

7

Chapter II

Barometers of the Mind

Serenity pays large dividends in physical health. The emotional tone of the mind probably has more effect upon the function of the body than any other single factor. The mentally disturbed are not simply sick in the mind—they are ill all over. This is a condition not confined to severe cases. Millions of normal people suffer from chronic ailments that are the result of the emotional pressure under which they live and work.

Doctors variously estimate that the ailments of sixty to eighty per cent of all their patients are directly caused by emotional conflicts. These patients are suffering from what is known as functional disorder. This means that there is nothing specifically wrong with the organs of the body. The way in which the organs function together is merely out of order. Over a long period of time improper functioning can produce permanent tissue damage. But members of the medical profession universally agree that if people could learn to avoid emotional conflicts, a very high percentage of physical disability would be eliminated.

It will help us to maintain serenity and better physical health if we understand the close connection between the two. Everyone needs to become better acquainted with the way in which his body and his emotions work together.

The inter-relationships of the body's cells are so complex that a disorder of one organ can seriously affect the entire organism. On the other hand, considering the body's marvelous equipment, it is surprising we ever become ill.

The ordinary person does not know how to manufacture

adrenalin, but the cells of his body know how. It requires skilled technicians and an expensively equipped laboratory to produce an antitoxin against scarlet fever, but the cells of the body know how to fight the disease. Man has never learned how to make red blood cells, but the tissue which we call marrow in the bones knows how to make them. Certain cells in the ear know what compounds to take from the blood stream in order to produce wax. Glands related to the gastro-intestinal tract take from the same blood stream the elements necessary to produce hydrochloric acid. These and hundreds of other chemically complex compounds are being produced continually within our bodies.

Modern man has become so familiar with illness and the symptoms of illness that he discounts the ability of the physical organism to conduct its business in an orderly fashion. Each of the millions of cells within the body knows instinctively what is needed to maintain its own health. The nervous system is a complex interrelationship of communication that automatically integrates all of the many functions required to keep the body strong and healthy. Every change in external temperature sets in motion a complicated procedure which maintains the body temperature of the normal individual at a constant level. The bio-chemical process of digestion goes on twenty-four hours a day with no conscious thought on the part of the individual.

All of this hidden knowledge is contained in the body's cells at birth. The physique of the normal infant is a rugged structure.

From the time of birth, however, the human organism is subjected to emotional pressure. Awareness of the external world begins to affect the functioning of the body. If physical, mental and emotional growth progress together harmoniously, the individual will retain the innate ability to maintain physical health. It is when the mind and the emotions fail to keep pace with physical development that the body's functions are deranged or disturbed by a lack of harmony.

When mental conflict reaches a certain severity, the

body can become ill through the effects of nothing more than emotion. A young woman sat in my office a number of years ago, describing her symptoms. She suffered from chronic fatigue, severe insomnia, sinusitus, headaches, swelling of the hands and feet, a breaking out on the skin of her hands, spasm of the gastrointestinal tract, heartburn, nausea, and pains under the heart. The function of the digestive apparatus was so badly disturbed that her normally slender waist was greatly distended. In addition to these physical symptoms, she told how she suffered continually from irritation in the presence of people. Occasionally she experienced periods of violent anger during which she felt her emotions almost completely out of control. These temper tantrums were frequently followed by a feeling of faintness when she sometimes collapsed weakly on the floor.

Before coming to see me, she had been examined thoroughly by a competent physician, who had told her that there was nothing organically wrong with her body, but that she was close to a nervous breakdown. He gave her some sedatives and recommended that she see someone for psychotherapy.

All of her symptoms were caused by emotional conflicts. After a few interviews it became clear that her problems had begun on her honeymoon. Childhood immaturities had been triggered by her reaction to the responsibilities of marriage and the experience of sexual intercourse. After she had discussed these problems rather thoroughly, she was able to revise her emotional attitudes with the understanding help of her husband. Her severe symptoms all disappeared in about six weeks and she has never had a recurrence of her difficulty.

This example illustrates how completely a physical organism can become disordered by a few relatively minor emotional conflicts. Fortunately, most people will not have just the combination of tensions to produce so many physical symptoms. Nevertheless, great numbers of normal people spend years visiting physicians for minor ailments which could be cured rather simply if they only understood their own emotional attitudes well enough to correct the basic difficulty. Perhaps we can better understand the effect of emotional tension upon the body by performing a simple experiment.

Hold your hand out before you, palm up. Now clench your fist as tightly as possible for ten or twelve seconds. Relax the fist and look quickly at the palm of your hand. It will be covered with red and white splotches where the closing of the fingers has interfered with circulation. You will also notice that your hand had begun to feel cramped.

You have just seen the result of sustained muscular tension. The improper circulation of blood in the palm of the hand was caused by the conscious flexing of muscles in your arms and fingers. No permanent damage was done to the tissue because you relaxed the tension after a few seconds. Suppose, however, that chronic emotional tension has produced a more or less continuous muscular spasm in any part of the body. Having observed the effect of muscular tension on the palm of your hand, you can well imagine what continuous pressure of this kind can do to any organ so affected.

To use another example, if your work requires that you sit in a cramped position all day at a desk, you may find at the end of the day that you have little bunches of sore muscles close to the spine between the shoulder blades. The muscles are sore, not because they have done any particular work, but simply because a cramped position, perhaps coupled with emotional pressure, has caused them to remain in a state of unnecessary tension over too long a period of time.

Most people believe they are relaxed when they are actually quite tense. They become so accustomed to flexing their muscles uselessly that they have no real idea of how much energy they are wasting during the day.

Now let us turn our attention briefly to the mechanism by which emotional conflict can produce unnecessary disturbances in the functions of the body. The involuntary muscles of the body operate with no conscious thought on our part. Blood pressure, for instance, is controlled by the contraction and the relaxing of the muscles around the

11

hollow tubes we call veins and arteries. When we are excited, the blood pressure rises. The muscles of the heart increase the rate of the pulse. Other muscles in the gastrointestinal tract slow down their action so that more blood will be available to the large voluntary muscles of the body. Some of this blood rushes to the brain, speeding up its action. Excitement is an emotion. It expresses itself in thousands of tiny changes in the muscular tension throughout the body. This is a normal and necessary function. Suppose, however, that the mind is producing two conflicting emotions simultaneously.

Consider the circumstances of the young lady whose case we discussed a little while ago. She was deeply devoted to her young husband. She loved him very much. She wanted nothing more than to be a good wife and a mother. However, because of early childhood training and experience she found herself repelled by the necessity for sex relations. Thus two emotions, directly in conflict with each other, dominated her mind. She wanted to express love, and yet was afraid of the physical expression of love. Inwardly she felt pulled in two directions at the same time. Love and revulsion are incompatible. To these two emotions a third was added—guilt. Because she wanted to be a good wife and found herself inwardly rebelling against that which she considered to be her rightful duty, she began to experience strong feelings of shame accompanied by a sense of failure as a wife. Through the complicated glandular and muscular interrelationship of the body each of these emotions produced its own particular muscular tension. The central switchboard of the brain, known as the thalamus, was sending a whole series of conflicting messages to the muscles of her body. The thalamus controls all of the involuntary muscles. The task of the thalamus is complex, but the principle upon which it operates is extremely simple. The conscious mind sends a message to the thalamus in the form of an emotion. Immediately the thalamus translates these emotions into a series of appropriate signals directed to the body's organs. Love is one emotion. It demands a certain set of body reactions. Fear is another emotion. It has its own particular muscular patterns. Since the two emotions are in conflict, the body cannot express both of them at the same time without producing confusion within the body's cells.

As this condition persists, the function of the body's cells becomes disorganized. Instead of working together in a harmonious unit, they begin to oppose each other. Fatigue poisons begin to gather more rapidly than the cells can throw them off. In turn, the cells send messages back to the thalamus that the body is not functioning properly. The thalamus then forwards this message to the conscious mind in terms of a vague feeling of discomfort. The conscious mind, already filled with conflicting desires, is thrown into a further state of confusion by the upset condition of the body. The vicious circle continues until the individual learns to understand his own emotions.

Integrated emotions produce within the mind a feeling of well-being. Fear, jealousy, guilt and resentment begin to be replaced by love, joy, confidence and hope. The latter emotions produce a relaxed, comfortable body, in which the individual cells are able to express their natural intelligence in terms of normal function. *What* we think and *how* we think becomes extremely important if our bodies are to operate at maximum efficiency.

Good health produces a feeling of exuberance. The joy of the infant is very largely the result of fine physique. He lies in his crib and moves his hand or his toes. He laughs at the sheer joy of the physical sensation. He drinks his formula from the bottle. He burps and drops back into his crib for a sound after-dinner nap. The adult whose body is functioning properly experiences much the same kind of feeling. When a healthy man eats a hearty meal he experiences an inner feeling of well-being, resulting from the sensations of a gastrointestinal tract which functions like a well-oiled machine. The mountain climber, whose body is in condition, gets as much pleasure from the smooth proficiency with which his muscles operate as he does from scaling a peak. We do not fully appreciate the sheer pleasure of perfectly functioning cells until one day we suddenly become ill and are forced to spend some time in bed. As good health returns, and one is once more able to sleep at night and eat normally, he looks about his world with new eyes and says to himself, "How good it is to be alive!"

Thus, physical health and emotional maturity go hand in hand. When one feels well, he finds it easier to think right. When he thinks right, he inevitably feels better physically.

There is no man living who cannot improve his physical well-being by further developing his emotional stability. Disease may come—accidents may limit the capabilities of our bodies. These things will have their effect upon our health, but if we learn to think correctly we shall be able to eliminate a very large percentage of the ailments which afflict us.

As we learn to understand the connection which exists between emotions and physical function, we can often save ourselves from the return of serious emotional difficulty.

In avoiding the recurrence of a nervous breakdown or an alcoholic relapse, nothing is more important than learning to recognize storm warnings. Just as weather signs vary in different parts of the country, the warnings of an approaching emotional storm will be signalled by different symptoms from individual to individual. Warnings which herald a major emotional crisis for one person may only represent a passing mood for another.

In spite of these individual differences, there are some symptoms of emotional disturbance which are quite common among a great many people, regardless of their particular diagnosis. Learning to recognize these symptoms and knowing when their warnings should be heeded are valuable aids in maintaining an inner atmosphere of serenity.

It is just as important to *ignore* some changes in the weather as it is to give heed to those symptoms of change which indicate approaching tornado, flood or hurricane. A reliable barometer is a better tool for predicting storms than grandfather's old bullet wound.

The same principle applies if you must learn to take precautions against the more treacherous emotional storms before they wreck the carefully constructed patterns of serenity. In maintaining a strong resistance to these storms you will possess a great advantage if you have at your command a few reliable tools for predicting approaching emotional upsets. Your body's reaction to emotional pressure can often provide an excellent clue to the beginnings of emotional storms.

In order to use the function of any organ or set of organs as a barometer of the emotions, you should have competent examination by a physician to determine whether any organic condition might be responsible for your physical symptoms. Many identical symptoms can be caused by either emotional conflict or by organic conditions. Therefore, medical advice is necessary to determine whether physical symptoms are the result of organic disease or whether they indicate chronic emotional conflicts.

When a person is ill he should not attempt to diagnose himself. Many physicians have moved their places of residence to the cemetery because they thought they knew enough about medicine to diagnose their own ailments. They probably knew enough about medicine, but people have a way of losing their objectivity about themselves when they become ill.

If this is true for physicians, how much more should it apply to those of us outside the medical profession! If you have physical symptoms that are disturbing, do not dismiss them lightly. See a doctor in whom you have confidence and follow his prescribed treatment. If he says your trouble is "in your head" or if he is more understanding and recommends that you see a psychiatrist, by all means see a psychiatrist.

After you have learned from these professionally trained people how to distinguish the physical symptoms that are caused by your emotional tensions, you will have acquired a valuable barometer of your mental condition. *Until you have done these things, do not attempt to follow any of the further suggestions in this chapter.*

There are two further words of caution. First, if after your thorough physical examination and after your discovery of how emotions affect your body, you later develop some new symptoms, go again to your doctor for an examination. Second, *watching the barometer constantly can also be a symptom of unsound thinking.* The individual who is inclined to exaggerate his illnesses needs to be cautious in how he uses the body's symptoms as storm warnings.

Provided there are no serious organic problems, infections or glandular disorders, and assuming that a person secures sufficient rest and adequate food, the body of one whose emotions are well-balanced will function almost perfectly. In such a person, a sense of physical well-being will indicate that body, mind and emotions are functioning in a harmonious relationship.

Now, I am assuming that you have seen your doctor. Perhaps you have also had numerous consultations with a psychiatrist. Through the professional help of these people you have gained a fairly clear understanding of the emotional causes underlying your strange array of physical symptoms. Through your own experience or the experience of friends having similar problems, you have a first-hand acquaintance with what it is like to shake on the outside and to feel tremors inside the body. You know that chronic fear can dry up saliva until the mouth feels as though it were stuffed with cotton, and eating becomes impossible. You know about skin rash, perspiration on the palms of the hands, palpitation of the heart, choking sensations in the throat, cold sweats in the night, gastritis, poor circulation and periods of dropping blood pressure. You know the connection between emotional tension and chronic fatigue. You have found that continued muscle tension can cause headaches or pain in the muscles between the shoulder blades. Some of your friends may have described the peculiar constrictive feeling of a band around the head which accompanies certain emotional states. You have learned that there is almost no part of the body and no physical function which is immune to the effects of emotional conflict.

Your problem today is how to profit by this knowledge so that you can maintain maximum serenity, coupled with the maximum in physical well-being. If you are to maintain a mental equilibrium in the day-by-day business of living, you cannot be running every half a day to the psychiatrist. For the most part, once your course is set upon a solid understanding of the self, it is going to be your responsibility and yours alone to maintain that equilibrium. You can best do this if you are well acquainted with your own body and mind. Then you can deal with your own minor difficulties, facing problems honestly, in a manner best calculated to correct the causes of any daily upsets which may occur.

The mother of a very close friend is critically ill. Physicians attending the case say that death is near and they can offer no hope for recovery. This is a woman in her middle fifties, but on her death bed she appears to be seventy. Her doctors can describe the organic changes which began a few years ago as mal-function. Perhaps ten or even five years ago she could have corrected the condition by changing her way of thinking, but now it is too late. Organs of the body have been radically altered by continued malfunction. Her condition has become irreversible. Close friends who know this woman well are quite aware that her muddled thinking is killing her. This is a tragic example of something which takes place in hospitals and clinics across the country every day in the year. It is an example of the choice which life gives each of us—grow up or die.

People in such a situation are not bad people. They are merely individuals who failed to recognize the need to look within themselves for the cause of their difficulties. The laws of the universe regarding mental and physical health are as unchanging as the physical forces which control the material universe. These laws operate whether we have the right ideas about them or not. We may have the wrong explanation for certain things in our world, but our wrong explanations do not change the facts. Life's laws do not wait for our knowledge to discover them or become aware of them. We do not make the laws. It is important for our survival that we find the self-honesty and objectivity to discover the right answers about ourselves and our universe.

17

If we can learn to conduct our lives and our thinking in such a way that we will conform to the laws of growth in the universe, then we will achieve an ever-increasing harmony with life and an ever-increasing peace of mind.

There is an old saying that the universe runs in a certain grain and if one persists in going against the grain of the universe he gets splinters. We can discover the harmony of nature within our own bodies and within our minds. This is the area where each of us can best become acquainted with the universe. We will find that we have less fatigue, that we are able to produce more work, that we can feel well with less sleep and, to a much higher degree, we will be able to eat what we like without producing digestive disturbances. The body and the mind will become increasingly relaxed. The tensions of the external world will become less and less a part of our inner tensions. We will learn the truth of that old and well-known phrase, "Be not anxious for the morrow." If the mind learns to be at home with itself the body will be able to survive under the demands of modern pressures.

Any emotion which tends to produce intolerable tension and pressures within the human organism is a product of wrong thinking. *Any type of living, any philosophy of life, which adds to inner conflict is incorrect for the individual who harbors it.* Each individual must discover his own techniques for successful living. No individual will find his ascent to happiness by the same stairway as his neighbor. But the goals are the same, the serenity is the same, and the laws of growth which govern human life are the same for all of us.

As an example, one of the more common forms of emotional disturbance is known by doctors as "anxiety reaction." During World War II it was often called "combat fatigue." Symptoms include breathlessness, fatigue, palpitation of the heart, nervousness, irritability, chest discomfort, dizzy spells and faintness. The disturbance is accompanied by intense anxiety, described by those who have experienced the feeling as "the big fear."

18

An individual who has recovered from this emotional disturbance may find that a mild return of symptoms is occasionally felt. When this occurs, he should recognize the storm warnings promptly and take steps to correct the causes. His first reaction will probably take one of two courses. He will either panic and rush to a doctor for another physical checkup or, if the symptoms are mild, he will develop an alibi for his condition. If he yields to the feeling of panic, he should see a psychiatrist, not a general practitioner.

If, on the other hand, he can avoid panic, he will be inclined to blame the symptoms on circumstances. He should curb this tendency immediately. Instead of saying to himself, "My symptoms are caused by circumstances," he should say, "I am thinking wrong about something." It is not people, or problems, or pressures which cause the trouble. The symptoms are barometers of the mind, giving warning that old emotional habit patterns have reasserted themselves.

In seeking the point where the mind has dropped back into old ruts, one should ask one's self such questions as these:

1. When did the symptoms start?
2. What was I thinking at that time?
3. What old fears or guilt feelings are being aroused?
4. Who upset my "play party?" Who hurt my "little feelings?" From what "little boy" or "little girl" emotions am I suffering?
5. Of what am I afraid: failure? success? a future decision? disapproval of others?
6. Have I become self-centered about something?
7. Am I working with too much hurry or tension?
8. Or, am I trying to escape from some undesirable situation by getting sick?

These are the kinds of questions one should ask one's self. When one finds the cause of the emotional upset and corrects it, the symptoms will start disappearing. *A symptom is only a warning signal. It is not the central problem.*

The pain of a toothache can be endured briefly if one has an appointment with a dentist who will remove the *cause* of pain. One does not permit the symptom to panic him into unreasonable fear. The symptom disappears when the basic cause of the trouble is corrected. In the same manner, the emotionally disturbed individual must seek the basic difficulty. If one will get to the heart of his emotional tornado and straighten out his thinking, the body will quit flying its storm warnings.

Self-understanding is a prelude to equanimity for such a person. But to self-understanding must be added self-mastery. The mastery of one's own moods is not the least task in achieving adulthood. Perhaps self-mastery is not the right expression to use, since it implies a rigid control that is the exact opposite of the flexible strength identified with those who achieve peace of mind. Nevertheless, the choice for the troubled mind is quite clear— the man must control the emotions, otherwise, the emotions will dominate the man.

The ascent of the troubled mind to a higher level of sanity can be likened to the struggles of an inexperienced mountain climber. For a time he flounders in the entangling underbrush of his confusion. He wanders without direction in the smothering fog of his enormous fear. He is threatened by the predatory animals of his uncontrolled emotions or trudges hopelessly from day to day in a morass of depression to which there seems no end. Despair often fills the troubled mind. At other times, there is only confusion. Finally, through the help of an experienced guide, one finds the upward trail. Clarity of mind and a measure of happiness is restored through a newly-found method of living.

Those of us who have gone through such an experience look back to the unhappy valley of our recent misery and wonder how our thinking could have been so completely confused. We have climbed the first ridge of our

20

ascent. We feel that never again will we lose the sunlight of a clear mind. This is the first area of danger. The individual who is fighting his way back from the depth of mental confusion and the torture of unorganized emotion grows over-confident with the first feelings of success. Danger lies at that point where he is very sure he has all the right answers to his problems. The alcoholic who returns from the clinic saying, "Alcohol is no longer a problem to me," is closer to a relapse than he knows. Taking such an attitude upon leaving the clinic is the folly of ignorance for an alcoholic. He has been a very sick man. His condition is arrested, not cured. It would be just as foolish for the arrested tubercular patient to leave the hospital saying, "Tuberculosis is no longer a problem to me."

All of us find it easy to fall into this subtle trap of over-confidence. After we have climbed from the more critical areas of our despair and confusion to the point where we can grasp a small measure of serenity, it is quite natural to feel that all of our worst troubles are over. But, like the mountain climber who has mounted his first ridge, many difficulties lie ahead. There are yet many glaciers to cross, there are rocky ridges to climb before one is able to place his foot upon the upper levels of steady living. Those who have experienced the ups and downs of emotional growth know well that the threat of a fall is ever present. The rewards for one's effort are great, but the element of risk is present in all growth.

The first lesson we must learn is the fact that we are never more than one slip away from the possibility of a headlong plunge back to the depths. Without this knowledge our progress is always in danger of being lost. By using the barometers of physical symptoms we can often avoid these danger points. The fact that we once went over the brink into the chasm of inner failure should provide a knowledge that will make our remaining years the most satisfying part of our lives.

Chapter III

Replacing Self-pity
with Constructive Action

Every one of us indulges occasionally in self-pity, but no one likes to admit it. Self-pity is the emotion of covering up. It is a method we often use to cover up our feelings of aggression and our feelings of guilt. It is our excuse for failing to face life objectively—an alibi for inaction. It is the salve for our pride when we fail to take seriously that portion of the Alcoholics Anonymous Serenity Prayer which reads, "courage to change the things I can."

I well remember calling upon a young man in a midwestern city who had contracted polio some five years before. He had made contact with the vocational rehabilitation agency in his home city. The counselors employed by that agency had met with no success in getting him to train himself for some occupation whereby he could become self-supporting. He was about twenty-one years old—an only son who lived with his widowed mother. The rehabilitation people felt that perhaps it might do some good if I, being a polio, would go to his house and talk with him about his problem.

Of course, I went. It was a hopeless case as it stood at that time. I found that the mother, in her desire to feel that she was needed by her son, had completely sold him on the idea that he was a helpless cripple. Actually, his possibilities for mobility were greater than my own. At that time I was on crutches and driving an automobile. I was holding a full-time job with a business concern in the city. But this young man spent most of his time in

22

the wheel chair, only occasionally getting on his crutches. He politely but firmly resisted any attempt I made to encourage him in the belief that he could do something occupational. His mother had convinced him that he was an object for sympathy. He was a very fine, intelligent young man with a pleasing personality, but my attempts to get through with any suggestion of decisive action were met with the kind of resistance one would feel if he were up against a wall of yielding, spongy rubber.

While this is an extreme example of what self-pity can do to a personality, we see, on a smaller scale, the same kind of results every day in lives of people all around us—people who are unable to take decisive action because they feel their difficulties are the result of circumstance. They can see no possible way in which their lives can be changed for the better.

In order to get rid of self-pity and replace it with positive, constructive action, we must first find out why we feel sorry for ourselves. Self-pity has many roots. One is the self-love characteristic of the little child, who feels that he is a center of the universe. In this form self-pity is a bid for attention. The individual who indulges in such self-pity feels that nobody loves him as much as he would like to be loved. Therefore, he will love himself. It is self-pity of this sort which is expresed in the old doggerel verse:

> I wish I wuz a little egg, away up in a tree;
> I wish I wuz a little egg as bad as bad could be;
> I wish a naughty little boy would climb up after me;
> I'd bust myself all over him and splatter he with me.

We all have mild impulses of this kind when we feel we have not received the proper amount of attention, affection or appreciation. Such attitudes prevent us from becoming the persons we are potentially able to be. When we harbor these feelings over a period of time we become capable of taking some inconsequencial slight, some uncomplimentary word, and developing it into a fine, monumental grievance toward life.

It is typical of the negative emotions which cripple

our mental attitudes that they are always small and subtle in their beginning. We see in this bit of so-called poetry the suggestion of self-pity as a cloak for aggressive tendencies. Often people whom we imagine are meek, mild, quiet, long-suffering types are individuals who, beneath the surface, have murder in their hearts. They are loaded with aggressions. They feel that life has imposed upon them, that people have taken advantage of them. They would like to strike out at these circumstances and these individuals. But for one reason or another, they are afraid even to express verbally their hostile feelings. Consequently, they bury these feelings deeply, cover the grave in which they buried them with the earth of self-pity and decorate it with the artificial flowers of a false humility.

The community is often surprised when such individuals break out in a rash of hostile action, after having suppressed their feelings of aggression over a long period of time. People may exclaim, "I never would have thought it of him. He always seemed such a nice young man."

We sometimes confuse niceness with goodness. The world is full of people who have nice exteriors. Only as we come to know them better do we realize that they are frequently loaded with self-pity, under which lie strong feelings of aggression.

This is a typical attitude among many alcoholics' wives, who have been told by the community that they are such sweet, kind, little things, because they are so forbearing with their problem husbands. Underneath, the wife sometimes wishes her husband would drive the car into a telephone pole on the way home from a drunk. Of course, it is not proper to have this kind of feeling toward one's husband, so the wife feels guilty about her thoughts. She excuses her failure to take any decisive action by saying that life has been cruel.

There are other roots for feelings of self-pity. For instance, the futility and frustration felt by families of

24

alcoholics during a long period of unsuccessful attempts to battle against the effects of the problem often drives them to feel sorry for themselves. Members of the alcoholic's family have found that all their positive efforts are geared to maintaining a public front. Their minds are often filled with fear and confusion. They are caught in a web of circumstances over which they feel no control. In the isolation of aloneness, self-pity becomes an easy antidote or compensation for both insecurity and guilt feelings.

Families of emotionally disturbed people often wonder whether they are somehow to blame for the illness of their loved ones. Yet, at the same time, they feel that the inconvenience and disgrace involved in any emotional illness partially balances the nagging sense of guilt and self-doubt. It is a well-known fact in psychology that men and women with tendencies toward self-pity are often individuals who find unconscious satisfaction in having to endure home situations where they will receive abuse and be placed in the position of a martyr.

A good example is seen in instances where alcoholic husbands have obtained sobriety only to find that their wives have developed a deep-seated resentment against the husband's resumption of his proper responsibilities. Such wives are resentful because they are no longer able to express their need to be the center of the universe in the home. During the drinking days they could ward off feelings of insecurity by the knowledge that the welfare of the home and the children depended wholly upon them. At the same time, they could feed their hunger for love by occasionally pitying themselves. After the husband achieves sobriety this uneasy balance of psychological needs is upset. Time is required to place the emotions upon a more mature and satisfactory basis.

The children of the alcoholic will be envious of their schoolmates who come from happy homes. They are haunted by a sense of shame. They are afraid to invite friends to the home, for fear father may come home drunk that night. Self-pity often rides heavily upon the young shoulders of children raised in an alcoholic's home.

Related to this root of self-pity is the difficulty which sometimes occurs when one is exposed to conditions or difficulties from which no desirable escape seems possible. It is all very well to say that the wife of the alcoholic "should leave the bum," but the wife of the alcoholic with five children and no money, with only her occupational skill of housekeeping, may find that the hell of living with an alcoholic is no worse than the possible hell of divorce and having to support the family herself.

It is true that life is never without hope, but the fact remains that in real life some situations are more hopeless than others. So, when one disaster is piled upon another, it becomes easy for any of us to believe that the cards are stacked against us, no matter how we shuffle them. Hopelessness can crystallize into chronic self-pity. Self-pity, in turn, produces a greater inability to take decisive action, even regarding smaller decisions. Thus a vicious cycle of frustration, aggression, inaction, self-pity, and more frustration is set up.

Another root of self-pity is found among those who are so afraid of failure that they find it necessary to exaggerate difficulties into impossibilities. For practical purposes such unfortunate people are unable to attempt anything which might involve the risk of failure. They excuse their dilemma by reminding themselves of life's difficulties—how helpless they are to confront the daily problems of living.

We sometimes find that self-pity is adopted by those who feel there is no real purpose in life. They keep asking themselves, "What is the use of living? What purpose is there in human life anyhow?" They are really asking a very selfish question. They are not asking, "What is the purpose of the universe?" but rather, "What purpose is in it for me?" This is a pointless question, since none of us can fully appreciate or realize our place in the total pattern of the life around us. When anyone of us asks himself the question, "What is the purpose of life?" with

26

a tone of self-pity, he immediately betrays the fact that he feels he is the center of the universe and its purpose must focus in him.

An illustration of whining and carping at the incomprehensible nature of the universe is found in one of the so-called wisdom books of the Bible, where the author starts out with the words, "Futility of futility, all is futility." He then goes on to explain how he has tried everything, has done everything, experienced everything and there is no point in any of it. He sees his everyday life as a dull round of eating, sleeping, working and going through the daily routines of living. He apparently is not desperate enough to drink himself to death or commit suicide, but we have the feeling that he might just as well.

This attitude was expressed a few years ago by a young twenty-year-old, who committed suicide and left a note in which he said, "I have experienced everything, there is nothing more for which to live." He thought that he, as an individual, was a receptacle and a center for all the experience of life and, like all people who center their lives in themselves, he found that there was nothing important enough to warrant continuation of the self. So he committed suicide.

Self-centered feelings are found within the individual who tells you that he is going to drink himself to death. An individual, with whom we worked in our alcoholic rehabilitation program, recently told the counselor that he planned to get drunk every week end for the next four years and then he was going to die. Naturally, with this kind of attitude we are not able to do anything in the way of rehabilitation or therapy for him. On last report, he was doing a good job of carrying out his announced plans for the next four years. It is all very well to say that he must have experienced many discouraging difficulties and problems in his life, which is true. But he is also a victim of his own negative emotions, of which self-pity is one.

How do we get rid of this kind of horrible, vicious cycle? As is the case with all negative emotions, we must first *admit* that we have an attitude of self-pity. Then we must recognize that the problem is within ourselves, instead of in external circumstances. We must realize that the harboring of self-pity is fatal to success in solving any difficult problem. Our difficulties are not the making of circumstances or environment, but the result of our own reaction to those circumstances. No one likes to face these facts, but it is an essential step if we are to overcome feelings of frustration and indecisiveness.

I would like to take another illustration from my own experience with polio. When I first contracted the illness, I realized that if I were to permit myself to indulge in self-pity over the things that I could not do, that my own strength would not permit me to adjust properly to the limitations of the illness. I realized that I was not strong enough emotionally at the time to endure the effects of thinking about anything which I could not do. I made an agreement with myself that whenever I started to think about anything which I could not do, I would immediately replace that thought with a thought about something that I *could* do. I practiced this discipline for a period of a year. At the end of that time I was doing so many new things, and life had become so interesting, that I could then bear to think objectively about the things I *could not* do.

But, of course, by that time I did not wish to spend much time thinking about my limitations, as I had become much too interested in the things I was doing. This was my antidote for self-pity—an emotion which I knew I could not afford.

We have to take a tough attitude toward the immaturities within ourselves which make self-pity seem necessary. We need to get rid of false guilt feelings. We need to learn to express our aggressive feelings in *constructive* ways, but express them in such a way that we get them off our chests as quickly as possible. We need to understand the underlying causes of our self-pity and recognize this emotion for the thing it is—a way of avoiding possible failure by exaggerating difficulty to the size of impossibility. We must realize that our own self-pity, not the external problems, is our real obstacle. In the face of real problems which are temporarily unsolvable, we must discipline ourselves to think of that which is possible, to consider the limitations which life forces upon us with the question, "Within the framework of these limitations, what action can I take?"

A positive attitude is difficult for anyone who has been confronted with a problem for which there is no immediate solution. But we must learn, above all else, not to indulge in self-pity. We may not be able to correct the situation immediately, but we can change the attitudes we have toward it.

If you have been in the habit of vacillating from one opinion to another, you may not be able to make big decisions immediately. But you should get into the habit of saying, "Now, is this a problem I can solve? Is this something about which I can take action today? If so, what action?" Having decided upon some positive course of action, take that step. Do not look back. Once you are convinced that a decision is right for you today, make your choice. You must face the fact that whenever you make a decision, you also rule out other courses of action which may seem good to you. But this is the essence of decisive living. Man is ultimately and finally revealed in his choices. When the situation seems most hopeless, it is most necessary to be decisive, rather than to indulge in the self-conceit of one's own self-pity.

I am reminded of a poem written by Bjornson, called "Strength". This poem has been of great help to me in anxious hours of crisis:

Rejoice when thou dost see
God take thy things from thee;
When thy props are laid low
And friend turns to foe.
'Tis but because now
God seeth that thou
No longer on crutches must go.
Each here
Whom He setteth alone,
He Himself is most near.

Often we feel that our props are laid low, that we have lost everything which is worthwhile. When that time comes, when we reach bottom—the bottom of our own resources—it is well to realize that perhaps the Higher Power is saying to us, "Now you must turn and face yourself and learn at last to walk on your own two feet." The universe is trusting us enough to do that.

When he learns to walk, the little child must take one step at a time. Even that one step is a faltering attempt. He always takes the risk of falling, but until the child learns to walk he does not become discouraged when he loses his balance. He gets back upon his feet and tries again. Gradually his muscles strengthen and the ability to balance increases. The child learns to walk with confidence, with head erect, rather than half bent over in a position where he expects to fall on his face. In overcoming negative emotions, which limit our lives, we must have courage to stand erect and patience to take one step at a time, recognizing that growth takes time. Even after we have taken positive action, it is easy to revert to the old, negative emotions. We should not cease to try because of a fear of falling.

The best way to face any difficulty or limitation is to learn how to use it. Life is full of many experiences —some of them good and some of them bad. The art of graceful living, the art of mature living, is largely that of learning to utilize both the good and the bad in a positive way.

We often hear the facetious remark among alcoholics,

"No drunk is a hopeless case. He can always be a horrible example." There is a grain of real truth in this. No one's life is actually wasted. We can always be an inspiration in the things from which we have recovered. The mature man or woman is the one who bears the scars of many battles, who stands upon his feet in the sunlight of truth and self-knowledge, unashamed of the scars, the hurts and the bumps, saying, "I may not be very far up the road, but this is progress which I have made today. My life today, compared with the mess it was yesterday, shows progress. As the days come and the days go I will continue to progress and grow into a greater ability to be decisive, rather than permit myself the defeating luxury of SELF-PITY."

Chapter IV

Accent the Negative

It is an unflattering commentary upon the human race that millions of people never learn the satisfying art of being serenely decisive. Their choices never quite seem to fit their real needs; or else they carefully avoid situations in which it is necessary to make strong, irrevocable decisions. Floundering without direction along the twisted, uncertain trails of life, they struggle against the tangled foliage of their own frustrations, blaming their confusion upon unfriendly circumstances. They vaguely wish for a different kind of life more nearly like their ideals, but are somehow never able to achieve the techniques of decisiveness without which nothing can be changed.

To face life with decisiveness is one of the most important achievements of emotional maturity. Conversely, the deeper the emotional confusion, the harder it will be to make constructive decisions. When the mind is sufficiently incapacitated by emotional conflicts the most uncomplicated decision will seem impossibly difficult. I have had women clients who were unable on some occasions to decide whether to wash the dishes or make the beds. The necessity for making this kind of simple decision was too great a choice. They would sit in a semi-daze for an hour or would wander aimlessly about the house until they could get their minds reorganized sufficiently to make ordinary choices. I have seen men so badly disorganized that the familiar task of driving an automobile was a terrifying prospect. They simply could not bear the thought of choosing which control on the instrument panel to move first.

These examples are somewhat extreme to be found outside a mental hospital, but they serve to illustrate the fact that emotional conflict can occupy a very large part of a person's mind. To phrase the problem in a rather facetious manner, if only two brain cells are free to function productively, the most simple task will be impossible.

Even after the mind has been freed of its bondage to conflicting emotion, longstanding habits of indecisiveness need to be replaced by exercises in the ability to make choices. Man is endowed with freedom of choice, but if he is to possess the land of his inner freedom he must make use of his endowment.

Decisiveness is ten per cent knowing where one is going and ninety per cent learning to say, "No." The art of saying, "No," very sweetly, but very firmly, is the mark of the individual who is confident of his direction and determined to let no minor considerations divert him from his course. So much emphasis has been placed upon thinking positively that we often fail to accent properly the necessity for quiet firmness in saying, "No." A series of feeble assents to half-hearted choices often indicates indecisive vacillation.

Knowing the right course for one's self is the first step toward growth in decisiveness. Anyone who has been forced by the demands of an adult world to straighten out his own twisted thinking has found that even simple decisions are often monumental crises. A person with a confused personality will never undertake difficult tasks unless life has slammed him up against the hard wall of circumstances—until his health, his job, his family or something important to him is threatened with total wreckage. Recovery then requires self-honesty and a pitiless search for the truth along the tortuous paths of the mind.

No one likes to admit that his personality is badly out of focus—that it needs the kind of repairs demanded by emotional illness. No one likes to face the necessity of reconstructing his life. For one thing, pride stands in the way. Another obstacle is the rigorous mental discipline which recovery demands. However, as one learns greater self-understanding, one takes new pride in the ability to choose one's course. The second step is that of developing the techniques for expressing decisions in action.

Many people have found the so-called "serenity prayer" from the pen of Reinhold Niebuhr an aid to decisive living. This prayer is often quoted by members of Alcoholics Anonymous. The words not only accent a simple appeal to a higher power; the serenity prayer is also effective because it defines a three-point technique for establishing decisive thought in everyday affairs.

> God grant me the serenity
> To accept the things I cannot change;
> Courage to change the things I can;
> And wisdom to know the difference.

Before we discuss the ways in which this simple formula is applied to daily decisions, there is another consideration which is basic to the habit of decisiveness.

No one is truly prepared to face life until he is ready for death. No one is properly equipped to expand his possibilities until he has faced the reality of his own human limitations. There is a marked difference between knowing how to embrace life and the desire to cling desperately to it.

Happiness is not achieved by a frantic search. Peace of mind eludes us when we pursue it with struggle and with tension. Even health cannot be gained by concentrating all our attention upon the body. The hypochrondriac does that. He makes himself ill by continually trying to be well.

What has this to do with learning to be decisive? Everything. Successful living is a balance between tension and relaxation. Successful decisions are made in an atmosphere where concern and disinterested objectivity are in a balanced harmony with one another. We achieve this delicate balance by learning not to cling too tightly to life. If you have made your peace with the possible calamities that life can bring, you are then free to relax and enjoy each day to the full. If you have honestly faced the possibility of the worst that can happen, you will not be afraid to make choices. Kipling has expressed this thought in the lines,

> If you can make one heap of all your winnings
> And risk it on one turn of pitch-and-toss,
> And lose, and start again at your beginnings
> ——————
> You'll be a man, my son.

We all strive to attain our ideals. We all seek security. Everyone struggles toward a perfection which is seldom realized. But the acceptance of limitations—the recognition that compromises are often necessary—is essential if our decisions are to fit the needs of everyday life.

This implies no surrender to life. In our youth we often confuse realistic compromise with surrender to circumstance. Youth is inclined to think that it can do anything. Youth wants to remake the world, accumulate a great deal of money, travel to the ends of the earth, marry the perfect mate and experience all things. Many of us have carried these castles of our dreams into our middle years, measuring our meager accomplishments by the yardstick of the stars, not recognizing that the control of life and its direction is far more important than a large quantity of experiences. To accept the inevitable is not a compromise of principle. As Max Ehrman wrote, "If I come not into the castle of my dreams, may the evening twilight find me gentle still." To know one's self is to recognize one's limitations. In learning where compromises are necessary we must also distinguish those points where compromise threatens principle.

This is the meaning of the first phrase of the serenity prayer, "God grant me the serenity to accept the things I cannot change."

The prayer then goes on to say, ". . . courage to change

the things I can." Compromise with the necessities of life is often necessary, but how often we fail to deal constructively with those circumstances which demand courageous action! We would prefer to drift and dream. We wait for a miracle to change that which we are afraid to meet with strength. We procrastinate. We dodge responsibility. We are often afraid to face the possibility of failure. It has been said that there is a time and tide in the affairs of men. A more facetious philosopher once said, "Grasp opportunity by the forelock; it is bald behind." Yes, we need to pray for courage to change the things we can.

To stay upon the path of emotional growth, one must be earnest enough to recognize that continued emotional growth comes *first*. Many people would like to have serenity. They would like to be successful and happy, but they strive for these things while clinging to patterns of behavior which add nothing to their growth. It may be necessary to seek new associates, new hobbies, or even a new occupation. To build a new life it is necessary to pull up many old roots. The transplanting will be difficult, but if new soil must be found to promote our growth, there can be no compromise.

Sometime ago I met a man who had struggled with the problem of alcoholism for more than fifteen years. Both he and his wife eventually recognized that they were alcoholics. This man and wife received treatment simultaneously at two different alcoholic clinics. After they returned from the clinics, they were wise enough to recognize that some radical changes were demanded if sobriety was to be maintained. To establish new acquaintances and break familiar ties with former drinking companions, they announced they would sell their home and move to another community. Thus, they committed themselves to a course of action which would assist them in breaking old associations and also place them in a location close to an Alcoholics Anonymous meeting place. Their action built a new pattern of decisive action regarding their problem. In making this choice they impressed upon themselves the intention to place continued sobriety *above all else.*

In carrying out decisions it is far more important that we learn to say, "No," than to say "Yes," to everyone. We are afraid to be negative for fear of what friends and acquaintances will say. We are fearful that people will think we are making a big issue out of a small item.

This is a particularly touchy problem when one has suffered from emotional illness. The desire for approval is strong. If all men speak well of us we feel secure. Our fears and resentments often cause us to do things which alienate the friendship of people. Still, we crave their approval and we are extremely fearful of being positive enough to accent the negative. How free and relieved we feel when we first discover that a decisive "No" brings greater respect and recognition from those who are really important to us!

Many so-called normal individuals go through life rebelling against the fact that their time is taken up with clubs, social activities and civic enterprises in which they have no real interest. They yield to the demands of these activities year after year, only because they are afraid of what the neighbors will think. They would do well to ask themselves which is more important, public opinion or peace of mind?

I had an interesting experience of this sort when I started to write this manuscript. In order to clear time for writing, it was necessary to drop several organizational activities in which I had previously taken an active part. Afterwards a number of friends told me privately that they wished they had the courage to cut down on their numerous group affiliations.

When one is first learning to be decisive, he is prone to search frantically for acceptable alibis by which he can justify his course of action to his friends and acquaintances. This is nonsense. If a line of action is vital and important to one's serenity or way of life, he should steer his course without apology. A friend or acquaintance may ask for an explanation of the decision. The most effective and satisfying explanation is simply to say, "I am doing this because I want to." No adequate argument can defeat such a statement. If there is an activity which one must eliminate from his life, it is folly to waste time on such a time-worn excuse as, "I don't have time." To such an excuse acquaintances will begin giving a variety of helpful suggestions to the effect that time should be made for trivia. But when one says simply, "I do not want to," that is the end of the matter.

Having taken one's courage in hand and made a decision to change certain circumstances, there should be no wavering and no looking back. One becomes increasingly adept at making decisions in this manner. His self-assurance will grow. Inner security will become more firm as one achieves greater power over his own destiny.

It is better to be decisive and risk the possibility of making some wrong choices than to sit on a decision and vacillate indefinitely.

The best way to counteract vain regrets about some decision of yesterday is to concentrate upon today. Some find it useful to rephrase the serenity prayer in these terms,

> God grant me the serenity
> To accept the things I cannot change *today;*
> Courage to change the things I can *today;*
> And wisdom to know the difference *today.*

To think in terms of today saves one from regrets about yesterday's decisions and avoids the impossible burden of trying to determine the proper course of action for all major decisions in the next year.

Decisive action today will not thrive in an atmosphere of anxious worry about tomorrow. If tomorrow seems to promise a hazard which can be eliminated by a wise choice today, then do what you can today. But do not live as though tomorrow were already here. A lady of my acquaintance has an excellent philosophy about past decisions which did not work out well. She smiles and says, "Well, it seemed like a good idea at the time." No vain regrets. No apologies to the past. No hesitancy about boldly deciding what seems wise today. The past is only valuable for the lessons it teaches. The future is only practical as a possible proving ground for those lessons. The present moment is where you do your living. Give today the best you have to give. Your efforts in the present will reward you by improving your past.

The final phrase of the serenity prayer asks for wisdom to know the difference between the things one should accept and the things one should try to change. This would seem to be the most difficult part of the prayer. No two people will apply the serenity prayer in the same way. It would be presumptuous to give advice to anyone on the basis of one's own experience. The choices we make are the most uniquely individual things about us.

Nevertheless, I should like to suggest something from my own limited experience with this prayer. When I am confronted with a possible course of action, I measure it against three major yardsticks:

1. Is it needful? Is it necessary to act, or would it be better if I accepted things as they are?
2. Is it true? Does it fit my own best self as I understand myself?
3. Is it kind? Does it consider the dignity of other people? Does it express love, integrity and consideration for others; or is it merely something by which I am giving vent to my own fears, resentments or insecurities?

These are my criteria. I do not always apply them as well as I could. But I find that when I try to follow these principles I live better than I would without them. I hold to the idea that it is better to aim at something good and miss it, than it is to aim at nothing and hit it.

In summary, we might say:

1. Be enough in earnest about emotional growth to make it the most important concern of your life.

2. Be willing to say. "No," to *anything* which interferes with that continued growth.

3. Attempt to be objective and honest in the selection of courses which best fit your new emotional pattern.

4. If the deeper self does not wish to do a certain thing, that fact is justification enough for not doing it. Each of us is primarily responsible in accounting to himself.

5. In following such a course of action, you will be amazed to discover that decisiveness earns the admiration of acquaintances, since most of them wish that they could exercise the same kind of courage.

In the process of growing up emotionally we will often be startled to discover vistas of new satisfactions opening up before us. We will begin to realize that our childish fears have kept us from enjoying freedom, that our desire for universal approval has made it impossible for us to gain the approval which we most desire.

These new satisfactions will not come all at once. Neither should we expect to plunge immediately into large decisions that tax our emotional strength too greatly. The first tentative steps will be the most important and with exercise greater decisions can be undertaken.

The great mountaineers begin their training by climbing little hills. In growing up, we must all learn how to walk before we can run.

Chapter V

Joining the Human Race

We all feel that we need the approval of others. It is normal to wish that our associates will consider us intelligent, attractive and capable. Unfortunately, some individuals labor under the intolerable burden of wanting the unqualified approval of *everyone*. They are upset at the slightest criticism or sign of being ignored. They not only wish to have the approval of their close friends, but also the enthusiastic commendation of everyone with whom they come in contact. They are miserable if they do not receive constant reassurance of being worthwhile and worth knowing. Life is a constant struggle to avoid all disapproval and criticism. As the climate of approval varies from day to day, there is a constant alternation between feelings of elation and depression. For the most part, such people are miserable. Even when they find themselves in the center of the stage of attention, their minds are obsessed with a feeling that the next moment will bring a signal of rejection.

Fears of rejection will continue to obsess those who fail to understand the basis for their social anxieties. It is a well known psychological fact that abnormal fear of social disapproval is usually linked with childhood experience. The wish for the kind of unqualified approval that can only be given to a small child by mother and father is carried over into adult life. The need for universal approval reflects insecurity, resulting from a need for love unsatisfied in childhood. Any criticism or any suspected criticism is interpreted in terms of rejection.

41

The fear of rejection may take the form of saying, "If you do not approve of everything I do, you are my enemy." On the other hand, some people may not have the ego strength to meet rejection with anger. The inner self may respond by saying, "If you do not approve of everything I do, I must be wrong in a great many other things which I also thought were right. If one thing is wrong, all is wrong. If you do not approve of everything, you approve of nothing about me." A great deal of weight is placed upon the opinion of others whom, in a normal state of mind, one would not consider as having much judgment. These attitudes indicate, in part, a failure to progress emotionally to a recognition of adult love as a two-way street. In the relationship between the small child and his parents love is a one-way traffic. The child is loved because he is small, defenseless and because he belongs to the parents' care. He contributes little toward that love except to coo and wiggle in a cute manner. The fact of his immaturity is accepted by his parents. They give their love to him, expecting nothing of him except that he continue growing.

As the child grows, however, he must learn to assume an ever-increasing share in family responsibility. The older he becomes the more necessary it is that he develop the ability to return love for love. If he fails in this development, he will retain a childish need to receive love without giving love. The need for unconditional approval in an adult is evidence of two things: first, an inadequate "diet" of love in early childhood and, second, a failure to grow into a realization that all adult love is experienced in sharing.

To seek universal approval as a substitute for love is not only an impossible goal, it leads to an undesirable kind of life. We sometimes exaggerate the importance of getting along with all types of people. We occasionally hear a man commended because no one speaks ill of him. *Ability to avoid all disapproval is more likely to indicate a putty-like personality than moral perfection.* It is not a compliment of character to praise a man for being blameless. The mature man tries to get along with everyone as well as he can; but he is not unduly upset if someone does not like the manner in which he "parts his hair."

The need for universal approval often displays itself in excessive suspicion of one's fellow man. The inwardly frightened person may feel that everyone is against him. He may appear upon first acquaintance to be quite a "hail fellow well met," but he is quick to suspect that individuals or groups are plotting against him. If he fails to secure the job promotion that he wishes, he suspects someone "had it in for him." Jealousy, suspicion and fear dominate this individual's life. When he is confronted with a difficult situation, he is never quite sure whether to cry or to fight. He is essentially alone in the world and is inclined to have a very low opinion of human motives. His overwhelming ego believes that other people have no purpose in life except to thwart his wishes. Since few people can give the unqualified adoration which he demands, he seldom finds any evidence to contradict his theory of persecution.

Failure to fit into group life also afflicts the individual whose chief motivation is the need to rebel against authority and conventionality. We observe excessive rebellion most commonly in rather strong individuals, who found it necessary during adolescence to revolt against parental authority. Their parents are apt to have been rigid individuals, who sought to build their own egos by dominating their children. The child could only succeed at becoming an adult by a violent declaration of independence from parental apron strings. The heartbreaks and personal tragedy resulting from a conflict of this sort can be disastrous both to the child and the parents.

Children who are brought up in strict religious homes quite commonly experience this kind of reaction. They enter adulthood with a strong need to prove their individual independence. Any type of authority asserted upon them later in life produces a counter reaction of rebellion. We have all witnessed the wastrel son who came from a home of pious parents. Conventional homes produce most of the Bohemian types. Rebellion for rebellion's sake is the foe of team cooperation. Many a small town boy moves to the city because he cannot face the demands which the smaller cooperative group of the village places upon him. Because he cannot adjust to the group, he brands its members prosaic, dull, stupid or uncouth. Any type of authority or social situation which reminds him of the home restraints will provoke a violent reaction. He may disguise this reaction with a variety of rationalizations and alibis, but it will lead him into all kinds of radical decisions which alienate him still further from the group life which he ardently craves.

These forms of social behavior are frequently found in those who cling to the childish need for being little centers of the universe. In effect, their childish self-love says to itself, "Nobody loves me, so I must love myself."

To achieve a sense of belonging, one must be able to understand these pressures within himself. He must take the little boy *within him* by the collar, set the child down on the chair and say to him, "Little boy, I know that you were hurt when you were little, but I am an adult and I am going to run my own life. I am going to quit taking orders from the irresponsible child within. I will not pamper you just because you were hurt when you were little." Anyone suffering from the problems we have described will find that the little boy inside will need frequent and repeated discipline.

In order to achieve a workable philosophy for belonging one not only needs to discover these things about himself, he will also find it necessary to achieve a new understanding of the social world in which he lives.

The art of getting along with other people has received a vast amount of attention during the past few years. Some things written on the subject have been good, but the reading public has also been exposed to much that is unadulterated nonsense.

Most of the books purporting to assist the reader toward better relationships with his fellow men fall into two main groups: success manuals and half-truthful Pollyanaish interpretations of the Golden Rule.

The success manuals state that the way to get ahead is to "sell" oneself to one's associates. We are told that the way to do this is to make the other fellow believe one is primarily interested in him. There usually follows several chapters with examples from the lives of "successful men" on various techniques one can use to fool associates into thinking one is only interested in them when actually he is using them to achieve his own purposes.

The books which give Pollyanaish versions of the Golden Rule as the secret of getting along with people make the assumption that if one loves everybody, everyone will love him in return. The thought is sometimes added that those who fail to love us after we have first loved them will suffer dire catastrophe.

Neither this approach nor the success-manual philosophy will help the emotionally upset individual who is seeking a real down-to-earth answer to the question, "How can I achieve a relation of togetherness with people?" The success manuals advise a smooth deceit which is the exact opposite of the self-honesty necessary to emotional maturity. On the other hand, the unrealistic interpretations of the Golden Rule overlook two facts: first, genuine love does not bargain with the universe on a return for its investment of love and, second, getting along with people on a mature basis certainly does not mean getting along with *everyone* in every situation.

Because we live in a so-called Christian country, we are told to believe in the myth that civilization is a pleasant pasture. According to this myth we are led to believe that good, loving and true behavior will induce our world to respond in a similar manner. This is not an entirely true picture of the civilization of which we are a part. Love has a very important function to perform in all human relationships, but like any other tool for successful living, love must be exercised with a true understanding of the world in which we live.

Civilization is a jungle. As adults, we must learn to accept the fact that all life is essentially a struggle for survival. The emotions of the child find it hard to accept this fact. Many adults keep looking for the green pastures of their childhood paradise. They continue searching for the childhood myth that life should be love and light and pleasantry. Like the jungle, civilization is friendly or unfriendly, as we make it. The jungle can yield a good life to those who understand it and use it intelligently. To those who cannot accept its hard realities, or to those who will not take the trouble to understand it, the jungle is a threat and a hideous green terror. All the essentials for a good life can be found in the jungle: fresh water, food, shelter and enjoyable diversion. But it also contains deadly reptiles, swamp fevers, fungus, and death.

The fact that many "predatory animals" within our civilized jungle wear tailored business suits does not change the fact that they are predatory. In the civilized world the threats to survival can be as real at a tea party as the terrors faced by uncivilized man confronted with the sabre-toothed tiger.

One can find friends in the jungle. One can know the serenity of peaceful days, and nights of restful sleep, but the jungle serves no pretty pastries on platters. Such is the society in which we live. Like it or not, we must live in it.

The mature man faces life with what tools he has at hand. With these tools he carves out of the jungle a little kingdom of peace in which he can find adult recognition. He attains a feeling that his efforts are worthwhile. He achieves the satisfactions which come to those who have learned to be tough without being brittle.

All those who would find a smooth path through the tortuous threats of today's society must be willing to give up childish illusions with the equanimity of a true adult.

Although it may seem to be a contradiction, one must

also achieve a proper understanding of love in the setting we have just described. Jesus said, "Love thy neighbor." He also said, "Do not cast your pearls before swine." To love does not mean to discard an objective viewpoint of life's realities. A great Christian leader once said, "The job of a clergyman is to kill himself, but gradually and intelligently." The business of getting along with our neighbors is not different for any one of us. In the jungle of civilization our task is to give of ourselves; but to do it intelligently and objectively.

The arts of giving and receiving are the greatest arts of life. We have heard a great deal about the art of giving, but the art of receiving is equally important. Achieving a proper balance between giving and receiving is a characteristic of the mature adult. Love involves a willingness to suffer and to be inconvenienced. True love is the art of giving with no thought of return. This is the exact opposite of those who love only to be loved, those who give only to receive, those who expect to purchase approval by a series of good deeds. We should give love in the same way that the sun gives its warmth. We should love because it is a part of our nature to love, just as it is the nature of the sun to warm the earth. Love's reward is in its function, not in what it hopes to receive from others. As love flows through us, we grow. If we give good things to life, we find joy in the giving, not in the approval which we expect to receive as a result.

How often we have heard the expression, "The more you do for people, the less they appreciate it." We do not give true love in order to receive appreciation. If appreciation and approval come as a result of our love, that is a bonus which is added to the reward which we already have through our love.

These then are the essentials for the achievement of a philosophy of belonging:

1. To know one's self
2. To know the world of people in which one lives
3. An understanding of the nature of love

47

A basic understanding of life is valuable only to the extent one develops techniques for putting it into action. Theories are necessary. But they will not get us through the stormy seas of troubled days unless the theories are expressed in action. As the late Arthur E. Holt so aptly said, "Theories are like the tail feathers on a rooster, highly ornamental, but not much use in a high wind." In the final analysis, it is the means we use to achieve our ends which determine our destination. In relationships with other people, we must develop emotional attitudes which enable us to meet our associates without expecting perfection in human relationships. Those who expect too much of others will always feel hurt or rejected by others. We do not expect perfection in ourselves. It is a ridiculous illusion to imagine that we can expect it in others. No human relationship will long endure if based upon the notion that every hour and day of the association will be perfect. Our closest friends will annoy us sometimes. Our dearest friends will say or do things which occasionally hurt or irritate us. Oddly enough, most of us are inclined to expect the most of those relationships which are most intimate. We often fail to realize that in an intimate relationship we learn to know each other so well that our faults are only too apparent.

We need to realize that what we define as perfection is usually nothing more or less than the reflection of our own image. We judge other people and their actions by our own individual notions of what is right and wrong behavior.

Strangely enough, most people suffering from emotional immaturities are perfectionists in the sense that they demand a pattern in human relationships which is a reflection of their own illusions about what is fit and proper in human behavior. Maturity demands that we recognize the essential democracy of life. We may consider that the other fellow behaves like a fool, but we must learn to give each and every individual the right to be a fool in his own fashion. If we cannot tolerate what we consider foolishness in others, we can hardly expect them to tolerate our own particular brand of stupidity. When we grow intolerant of other people it is because, in our egocentricity, we are setting ourselves up as judges of their behavior. Each individual should demand of life the right to be himself and he should grant to others the same privilege. This would seem to be an easy thing to do, and yet how often we say, "Now if I were you, I would do so and so."

The author well remembers a conversation which occurred between two patients in the mental hospital. One was an alcoholic and the other was a psychoneurotic. They were discussing their various problems and the symptoms of their respective ailments. The alcoholic had a keen understanding of other alcoholics but was completely unable to comprehend what he considered to be the foolish behavior of the psychoneurotic. The psychoneurotic, on the other hand, found it impossible to appreciate why the alcoholic felt that he needed to get drunk when he was confronted by intolerable pressures. To each individual his own irrational behavior seemed understandable, even though it was not commendable. One of the great bridges of human understanding is established when we achieve sufficient tolerance to respect other individuals, even though we cannot understand their peculiarities.

There is no serenity for the individual who feels that it is his responsibility to worry about what he considers the failure of others. It is always easy to assume responsibility for the problems and the failures of all humanity. There was the individual who, on some occasions, became ill for two or three days whenever he picked up a newspaper and read about the political scene in Washington, D. C. The news would literally make him ill because he felt that the men running the country were incredibly stupid. He could see nothing but disaster as a result of their actions. Basically, his mental attitude was an enormous conceit which said, in effect, "If I were in their shoes, I would know how to run the country properly." He achieved health and peace of mind only after he had cut his own ego down to size. He then recognized that his responsibility was only to himself. At that point he came to a realization that if he did a good job of living his own life, it would be a full time occupation.

It seems ridiculous that anyone could get himself in such a stew over affairs so remotely connected with his personal life, yet tension resulting from such emotional immaturities besets thousands of people to some degree. To detach one's self from responsibility for the actions of others relieves one of enormous tension. Almost any one can point out individuals during the course of a normal day whose intestines are upset and whose brows are furrowed because somebody in factory or office has done something of which they did not approve. How often has this happened to all of us! We need to recognize that the behavior of others is something outside ourselves. *If we become upset and disturbed by their actions, the tension is within ourselves.* Our real problem is not the behavior of others; it is our own tension. We must recognize the primary problem to be our own inner conflict. Millions of people go through life with a notion that they could have peace of mind if the circumstances around them were simply changed. They never realize that peace of mind is an inner state, dependent largely upon their own attitudes toward circumstances. Again and again we need to remind ourselves of this fact.

It is so important in human relationships to remember the thought expressed by Kahlil Gibran, "Let there be spaces in your togetherness." We should live together but not too close together. A sense of belonging can only be achieved if we learn to give each other room for privacy. The invasion of someone else's mind is only a method for building our own ego. There was a phrase common to the American frontier, "Tend to your own knitting." This is good advice. The stitches dropped by others are not our responsibility. Detachment and objectivity in our relations with other people will not be achieved simply by saying to ourselves that we must not worry about the other fellow. A positive approach is needed. If we will devote our thoughts *primarily* to conducting our own affairs as we relate ourselves to other people, we will find that our minds are so busy with this tremendous task there will be no time left to worry about concerns of others. The best way to rid the mind of an objectionable thought or habit pattern is to concentrate upon a new thought or habit pattern. If we wish to remove all the air from a glass tumbler, the best way is to fill the tumbler with water. A great many people vainly attempt to pluck the cobwebs of worry from their troubled minds, when all that is necessary is to fill the mind with constructive positive thoughts.

Our minds are often full of rubbish and confusion. We are accustomed by long practice to our unhealthy mental state. Old patterns will not be removed in a day. When one has spent years thinking incorrectly, he need not expect that a little self-understanding and two weeks' effort is going to correct the damage that required years to establish. A little mental discipline can be built each day, but it must be done each day. Old mental patterns will sneak back into the mind while one is busy in another corner correcting a second difficulty.

The day-at-a-time living recommended by Alcoholics Anonymous is notably effective in developing wholesome mental attitudes. It requires all of one's concentration to live each day to the best of his ability. Tomorrow one will need to repeat many of the things that he did yesterday. The procedure of concentrating on day-by-day living also keeps one so busy with the day's activities that he has no time to live in the past or the future. It is impossible to relieve anxiety by trying to stop worry. Nobody can stop worrying about anything. The only way to get rid of worry is to become absorbed in the present.

There is a passage in the Beatitudes which reads, "Blessed are the meek, for they shall inherit the earth." A better translation is that which is given in the French version. "Blessed are the debonair." To be debonair means to achieve a certain objectivity about life, which enables one to live serenely in the midst of people. One can then participate with appreciation in all that happens around him without completely identifying with any one individual or any one situation. To be debonair means that one takes his work seriously, but not himself. It means that one is well prepared to live because he is well prepared to die. "Blessed are the debonair," for they are prepared to live their lives to the best of their ability without overrating themselves. They are not overwhelmed by the tragic possibility of the termination of their own egos in death. To be debonair means more than assuming a jaunty air. As Kipling so well described in his poem, "If," it means possessing the ability to "meet with triumph or disaster and treat those two imposters just the same."

Various other habit patterns congenial to belonging can be developed by each individual according to his needs. Some of the following suggestions may be helpful:

Most of us would like to be good conversationalists but, unfortunately, we think the good conversationalist is an individual who talks all the time. Conversation is primarily the art of listening. It is a good idea occasionally to set the discipline of listening to an individual for an hour without expressing an opinion. We will discover to our amazement that we can keep a conversation going for long periods by simply looking interested and saying, "Uh huh, is that so?" or "Well, tell me more about it," at appropriate times. This is the technique of the psychiatrist. People will talk to us if we will listen. People love to talk, particularly about themselves. It is surprising how few people know how to listen without injecting their own personalities into the conversation.

Another good discipline is to try to get along for an hour in a group without once using the word, "I." This is a good exercise in keeping attention from one's self-centered interests. Learn to concentrate upon what people are feeling when they talk rather than in concentrating on what they are saying. React to their feelings, rather than to the facts and you will be surprised at the whole new area of human relations which will open up to you.

The author was once counseling a man who had a great deal of difficulty with his wife. They were about to get a divorce and the husband was desperate. The wife would not undertake any counseling interviews. As a last resort it was suggested to the man that in his conversations with his wife he adopt the policy of reacting only to her *feelings,* rather than the ideas she expressed. He did not really believe this would help, but he agreed to try it. When he went home in the evening his wife met him with the irritable remark, "Well, where have you been? Dinner's been waiting for ten minutes!"

Her husband replied calmly, "Do you feel that I should have been home earlier?" His wife launched into a tirade to the effect that he was always home late, she never knew where he was and he was probably stepping out with another woman.

Her husband heard her through calmly and then said, "Would you like to tell me how you feel about it?" He kept responding to her in this manner. In a short time she has blown off the pressure she was feeling and began to tell him about some of the real causes of her irritation. He continued to follow this procedure with his wife over a period of two or three weeks and was pleased to discover that he not only avoided quarrels, but that his wife's attitude began to change. For the first time in his married life he began to understand how she really felt. They are living happily together today—one of the best adjusted families in the community.

Learn to listen, and in the listening something will happen to you. Irritations and petty frustrations which so often spoil human relations will decrease and you will begin to discover that other people are almost as interesting as yourself. You will find that less and less do you need to feed your ego upon other people. The big "I" will not intrude itself so frequently in relationships that should be intimate. You will find less need to be moralistic and intolerant of other people. If you have been a show-off and the life of the party in every instance, you will find pleasure in sitting back and encouraging others to be the center of interest. You may find that you no longer take delight in the difficulties and the small disasters that befall other people. All of your inner attitudes will undergo striking changes as a result of your own increasing serenity and your sense of belonging to the group. If you have been one who has been in the habit of getting his own way by throwing a temper tantrum, you will discover more satisfying ways of getting attention.

All that we have said about learning to belong and all the many things left unsaid, which you will discover for yourself, can be summarized in the following rule: Do those things, say those things, think those things which will take you out of yourself. If you do this, you will find yourself.

Chapter VI

Modern Myths About Sex

Man's search for serenity is a quest for enlightenment about himself. The most puzzling problem we face is the riddle of our own minds. Nothing baffles us quite so often as the reasons for our own illogical behavior. The things we seek are not always the things which our actions produce. The complications of modern society have further tended to exaggerate the contradictions within man's own personality.

Modern man cries for peace while he prepares frantically for war. He yearns for equality of opportunity and, at the same time, shuts himself off from his fellowmen in little compartments of class and creed and race. He wishes for peace of mind, yet acts as though he were afraid of solitude. He likes to imagine that he controls his life by reason, while salesmen persuade him to buy their products with the psychological tools of "motivation research." Living in an age of unprecedented scientific and material progress, he often fails to recognize that his human relationships are unreasonable. This fact he hides from himself by elaborate group alibis. He does not wish to admit how irrational are many of his group relationships. These excuses for his behavior sometimes become so generally accepted that we can only refer to them as cultural myths.

Today's man views with scorn the superstitions of his Medieval ancestors. Yet the modern myths which dominate much of his thinking are hardly less ludicrous than those of previous ages. At no point is this more apparent than in the area of sexual relationship. The "goddess of love" has never been worshipped more devotedly or with more fanciful myths than at present.

If we are to gain any lasting growth in our sexual relationships, we must identify those mythical notions which cloud our vision.

There are four modern myths about sex which particularly hamper us in our search for wholesome attitudes. We shall call these false pictures of reality the myth of perfection, the myth of evil, the myth of strength and the myth of possession.

The Myth of Perfection

Each of the four myths finds wide acceptance among a large group of our American population. All of them distort the objective view of reality. Most of us have visited a "house of mirrors" at a country fair. Here one enters a room in which the walls are lined with various curved mirrors. In all of them one's reflection is strangely distorted. In some the image is drawn to a thin, narrow height. In others the figure is compressed to make one appear short and enormously fat. Our erroneous ideas give us a similarly twisted view of reality. When we view any part of reality through mistaken ideas we see an image of the truth which is as untrue as our reflection in an imperfect mirror.

We are unable to deal with our problems constructively because of our false notions about ourselves and our world. We are so accustomed to the distortions that we may even become incapable of recognizing the truth when it is presented to us.

The myth of sexual perfection is such a distortion. It deludes us into believing there is a thing called a "perfect" sexual relationship. The ideal of sex becomes a highly exaggerated goal. We are led to believe that we should be able to discover a mate with whom a complete fulfillment of all our dreams is achieved. The plot of this love story is always the same. Boy meets girl. They are fascinated by each other at first sight. An "electric" something passes between them and they are immediately in love. The courtship is an exciting whirlwind of ecstatic emotion. They are quickly married and they live happily ever after. We sentimentalize this plot in popular love songs and much of our current fiction.

Whenever a young couple attempts to build their relationship on this pattern the disillusionment usually follows quickly, for they have dreamed unwisely and too well. They have expected something impossible. They have distorted the image of reality with their dreams.

What passes for perfection is never achieved without struggle, effort and some pain. In any reasonably satisfactory marriage there will be occasions when a man and woman will experience happiness quite beyond description. There will also be wet diapers, dirty dishes, annoying irritations, pin curlers at midnight and dirty shoes tracking across a clean floor. There will be the tribulations of budgets, the sudden loss of a job, the unreasonable quarrel at the end of a tiring day.

If there is genuine love and a mutual effort at understanding and respect, then the sexual aspect of marriage will probably grow with the other growths of marriage.

On the other hand, a frantic struggle for so-called sexual perfection can only lead to frustration, impotence and frigidity. Sexual perfection sought in and for itself will bring disillusionment. Ardor of physical attraction will not remove the need for genuine sharing. A warm lover's kiss cannot substitute for agreement about a family budget or mutual understanding of what policy to follow in disciplining the children. Thoughtless and unkind words must be forgiven before the embrace of the marriage bed can resume its full meaning.

The myth of perfection asserts that a marriage is some kind of special human relationship where strong physical attraction will remove the ordinary problems of two people trying to adjust to each other. It is a misleading myth which ruins many marriages before they are past the honeymoon.

The problem is further complicated because no two people dream of sexual perfection in quite the same manner. Suppose the girl dreams of a sexual perfection in which tenderness is the keynote. If her husband's dream is composed of wild passion, they will both be disappointed. Both were expecting a certain kind of relationship. They were unable to see that these things must be allowed to grow. They did not really marry each other. They both married dreams and the dreams did not immediately materialize.

When a man goes to college he does not expect perfection of the roommate he chooses. Why should be expect perfection of the girl he marries simply because she is of the opposite sex? This precious little morsel of femininity which he marries is just as full of imperfections as himself. If he were choosing a roommate with whom to spend the rest of his natural life, there are certain qualities for which he would look. They are the same qualities he should seek in a marriage partner. If those qualities are present, the sexual part of marriage will generally take care of itself. No amount of high temperature sex can make up for tolerance, trust and enjoyment of another person's presence.

The real test of a sexual relationship is this: does one deeply enjoy the other's presence after sexual needs have been satisfied? Is it good, is it comfortable, is it pleasurable just to be around each other? Is each a better person because they are together?

In giving personality inventories to emotionally disturbed people it is surprising to discover how many men and women state the belief that the degree of sexual attraction is the best indication of good prospects for a marriage.

It would be foolish to suppose that sexual attraction plays little part in a happy marriage. But when we take one aspect of marriage—the sexual part—and exaggerate it to the point of expecting "perfection," we have seriously warped the substance of reality. We have not only placed undue importance upon one thing. We have also demanded that life must fit an impossible specification.

If we do this, disaster will result.

The Myth of Evil

No less troublesome is a notion which may be called the myth of evil. Those of us who have been raised in the Christian tradition labor under two thousand years of biased thinking regarding sexuality. This is not to say that *all* Christian thinking suffers from such a bias. But there have always been those in the Christian tradition who have believed that evil resided in the fact that man was born with a body.

From the vermin-encrusted hermits of the Egyptian desert, who mutilated their bodies in the mistaken notion that all physical desire was wrong, to the Puritanical missionaries clothing naked natives of the South Pacific in Mother Hubbards, we can trace this stream of biased thinking. It has only been within the last few years that some enlightened Christians have been able to raise their children without ingraining the fear that any slight deviation from the accepted patterns of sexuality would result in insanity, early death and the threat of hell fire.

To exalt purity of mind and motive is one thing. To debase the body which God created is quite something else. Those whose profession it is to provide psychotherapy for disturbed people find that at least half of all emotional conflcts are complicated by a kind of devoted, but mistaken, religious piety. There is something terribly wrong with child training when a whole adult life can be wrecked by guilt feelings caused by ignorant parental disapproval at a child's discovery of his genital organs when he was three or four years old. It is a curious kind of twisted thinking which defines purity as a denial of normal physical desire. This kind of so-called purity produces the nastiest variety of narrowmindedness. As someone has said, "To the pure all things are impure." We should remember that Jesus did not earn his reputation as a friend of publicans and sinners by adopting an aloof or intolerant attitude toward the more earthy members of society. He not only associated with these people because they sought his help. He also mingled with them because he knew they were apt to be honest and genuine. He preferred their company to that of individuals who imagined they were made holy by following a code of outward behavior without taking the trouble to clean up the sewers of their minds.

The purpose of guilt feelings is to warn us when our behavior is inconsistent with our inner ideals. However, guilt is not always the product of inner conviction, but sometimes the result of fear and insecurity. If early parental disapproval has been shown when a child was only exploring the mystery of his own body, these feelings of "being bad" may persist into the adult years. Thus, a guilty feeling can become more or less a chronic state of mind, unassociated with any specific act. Unfortunately, we not only pass on to our children the good things of our minds, we also convey to them the effects of our own guilts, insecurities and intolerant attitudes.

If we feel guilty about the mere fact of our physical desires, we will usually convey these same tensions and conflicts to our children. They will grow up under the ugly shadow thrown by our belief in the evil nature of our bodily urges. Why are we so stupid as to single out the one physical attribute of sex and call it evil? The man whose body craves food is not considered a transgressor of moral law when his mouth waters at the thought of a well-cooked steak. If his appetite leads to gluttony, he commits a crime against himself. The universe will punish him with obesity and physical deterioration, but the fact that man desires food is not evil.

Neither is the fact we are born with sexual desire an evil. We only transgress the laws of the universe when we *use* sex as an end in itself, as a means of getting rather than giving or as an indulgence of the self without due regard for the personalities and rights of others. Only as we recognize deep within our minds these facts of life can we avoid the substitution of a myth for reality. Only thus can we escape the intolerable burden of our false guilts and nameless fears.

The Myth of Strength

In our society a great many people seem unsure of their manliness or womanliness. This is an inner fear which, for the most part, they are able to conceal. Some of them frequently attempt to reassure themselves by proving they are sexually potent.

Undoubtedly there are many reasons why sexual ability has become an exaggerated yardstick of strength among the people of our culture. A great many thoughtful writers have given their opinions on this subject. Regardless of the basic causes, we find ourselves in a situation where it becomes important for us to recognize that manly and womanly strength are composed of other qualities besides sexuality.

This is made more apparent to us by two common observations. The first of these facts is noted by any psycho-therapist who accepts for treatment a middle aged man who complains that he is experiencing a sudden upsurge of vague fears and emotional tensions. The therapist is usually correct in his initial suspicion that part of the patient's problem is a fear of the effects upon his sexual capacity of the aging process. These fears have become so threatening to the patient that they have produced an acute anxiety.

The second fact is reliably noted by many physicians, who state that probably fifty per cent of all the men in America suffer some degree of sexual impotency during their lifetimes.

Both of these observations indicate that the male population has been exposed to ideas which exaggerate the importance of sexual potency and leave them with the fear that any temporary inadequacy in this area of living is a serious threat to their manly integrity. This is not a problem limited to men. The incidence of frigidity among women is also an alarming symptom that something is seriously wrong with our notions about sex.

Many psychologists are seriously disturbed by the current emphasis upon the female bosom. Even while this fad is in vogue, we find few mothers who nurse infants at the breast. Some psychologists have suggested that society tends to make an overly important sexual symbol of the bust because it has largely lost its original useful purpose. Other psychologists are disturbed by the current interest of ten and eleven year old girls in the early purchase of padded brassiers. They wonder about the emotional consequences to these girls as they grow to womanhood.

These are only a few of the indications that manly and womanly strength is identified in the minds of many people with the preservation of youth and the performance of certain sexual rituals. The result is a sexual myth of strength.

It is true that sexual vigor is more pronounced during youthful years. No one enjoys the prospect of increasing age and the necessity of adjusting his life to a decline of physical strength. The "fountain of youth" will always be sought as long as man survives upon the earth. Nevertheless, part of emotional maturity is the easy acceptance of natural aging without the feeling that glands make the man. There is no particular reason why we should measure manhood or womanhood by the activity of the sexual organs. As long as our bodies are functioning normally for their age and condition, we should learn to be content with things as they are. The things which make a man a man are his mind, his emotions and his character—not the size of his glands.

This myth, in which strength is gauged by sexuality, causes us to be afraid, to inflate the importance of youth and to create needless anxieties within ourselves. It is the basis for behavior which often proves the adage that "there is no fool like an old fool."

If we can only learn to accept ourselves as we are, rather than attempting to live by our myths, we shall have taken the first step toward freeing ourselves of our fears and insecurities.

The Myth of Possession

The myth of possession is the root of sexual jealousy. It leads us to confuse possession with love. Many marriages are ship-wrecked upon this rock. No man or woman has the right to feel that he can "possess" his mate. Love and loyalty are things which are given. They can never be possessed. It is true that when a couple are married they make certain promises to each other, but the act of giving love must be renewed every day.

In marriage many people assume that because a man in a black suit stood before them and pronounced certain words, that this act of the wedding gave them the right to be possessive. The words were "love, honor and cherish," not "possess, dominate and suspect."

Usually, individuals who confuse possession with love consider that the process of courtship stops with the wedding. The clergyman or the designated official performs the wedding. The marriage can only be effected by the man and the woman. The wedding takes a few minutes. The marriage requires a life time. The continuation of the love which should have been felt at the time of the wedding can only be possible if both the man and the woman continue to freely give love to each other.

Possessiveness is the enemy of love. If one partner begins to take the other for granted, if he behaves in a domineering and possessive manner, love will begin to die. He is violating the first principle of love—that love can only be *given voluntarily.* Too many women treat their husbands as though they thought, "This man is mine to mold as I choose. He exists solely to serve me, to support me, to pamper my whims." On the other hand, there are men who treat their wives as though they were property, as though the woman existed entirely to satisfy their

63

desires, to decorate the home, to care for the children. A woman so treated will soon feel that she is not truly loved by her husband. She will consider that to him she is only a convenient piece of furniture in the home. Love cannot grow in such an atmosphere. When there is love the two people will give themselves to each other, they will forebear with one another's imperfections. They will understand and forgive each other's failures.

If a man loves a woman and she is unfaithful to him, he will first ask himself, "Where did I stifle her love so that she felt the need to seek elsewhere for love?" If he cannot find the answer to that question, then he has only two possibilities consistent with his love for her. He can either let her go her own way, or he can reach an amicable understanding that they will share what companionship there is left to them.

The same thing applies equally to a woman who has lost the love of her husband. If both of them truly want the marriage to work, they will find a way to restore their love, to resume their courtship and to forgive one another.

The key words in marriage are not "my" and "mine." They are "ours" and "yours." In marriage one can only receive those things which are freely given in love. If one of the partners does not wish to give, there is no way that the other can compel him to give without further alienating the affections.

The myth of possession has its origins in an earlier day when a woman was regarded as the slave and the property of the man. Modern women will not accept such an arrangement. A very large number of wives assist in earning the family funds. Those who do not work outside the home consider themselves, and rightly so, to be the equals of their husbands. A man who insists upon inflating his own ego by treating his wife like a possession will probably do so at the price of losing her love, her respect and her devotion. If she happens to be one of those rare meek souls who suffers all indignities in silence, she will probably rebel inwardly at such treatment.

64

In such a case, the husband will lose contact with the most precious thing she has to give—the spontaneous sharing of her inner thoughts.

Any one of the modern myths we have mentioned is a foe of love and a barrier to satisfactory sexual relations. Fortunately, not everyone in our society lives under the delusion of these myths. There are many who recognize the true pictures of reality. However, those who have found difficulty in solving problems of sex and marriage will better equip themselves for the future if they recognize the false character of the myths by which their behavior has been governed.

All of the four myths we have mentioned tend to divorce love from sex. They are beliefs which make it difficult, if not impossible, to use sex as an expression of love. They distort the truth, they violate the sacredness of the individual and they prevent us from facing our real inner problems with honesty. They hinder us in our attempt to grow into the kind of people we are capable of becoming.

Chapter VII

The Mask of Deceit

The emotional patterns of one's life are reenacted in his sexual relationships. Whether a person is brutal, sensitive, frightened, self-centered or magnanimous, is usually mirrored in his love-making. In this most intimate of personal relationships, a major part of what we call personality will be revealed. Strengths and weaknesses of men and women are dramatized in the way they make love.

Not only are personality structures revealed by the patterns of sexual behavior, but men and women are also better understood when we know *why* they make love. Sexual attraction is based upon many things, of which physical desire is only one. Curiosity, emotional tensions, loneliness, and the desire for close identification with someone are a few of the reasons for love-making. Fear and anger may even play a part in temporarily heightening sexual desire.

No human relationship brings to focus so many complex emotional patterns as the expression of sexuality. No natural urge is subject to so many possible distortions. At the same time, sexuality offers us enormous potential for growth and emotional maturity. To achieve our fullest adulthood we must grow up sexually. Yet how few are the guideposts which are available to lead us toward such growth! The whole subject is often shrouded in a mist of secrecy and smut. Honest discussion of the subject is so seldom heard. What passes for sex education often leaves much to be desired. Many books which claim to help are either full of superficial pious advice or else they confine instruction to a listing of sexual techniques.

We are concerned here with the problems of those who seek to remove from their way of living some of the more troublesome distortions of sexuality—those who wish to find some clues to a more satisfactory sexual adjustment in which sex can be used as a partner of growth, rather than a satisfier of limited and narrow emotional needs.

There are four common distortions of sexuality which we shall mention. It will help us to understand problems of sex and suggest workable solutions if we first have a clear understanding of the peculiar twists ordinarily found among those who recognize their sexual problems. Until we have faced ourselves with rigorous honesty, it will be impossible for us to think clearly about any problem. The only tools we have for thought are our own minds. The individual who attempts to do any constructive thinking, without achieving self-honesty, will arrive at distorted con clusions. The mind of the individual suffering from self-deceit is full of little twists and turnings of which he is not aware. To attempt thought with such a tool is like taking a straight piece of wire and thrusting it through a coil of metal tubing. The wire will emerge from the other end coiled in the same shape as the tubing.

In no area of human life is a mask of deceit so carefully constructed as in the mind of the individual who misuses nature's gift of sexuality. The four misuses we would like to describe here are as follows: first, sex used as a means of aggression; second, as a means of reassurance and security; third, for the satisfaction of repressed curiosities; and fourth, as a method of rebelling against authority.

Sex Used as a Means of Aggression

Sex relationships are normally a method for the expression of love. Many people, however, use sex primarily as a means of expressing their anger. Consider, for example, the young woman of dominant personality who is raised in a home where her father is domineering, irritable, inconsiderate, and at times brutal. In such a situation it is very probable that the daughter will grow to womanhood with an intense hatred and dislike for the male. As she reaches adolescence, she may discover that by using her sex she is able to dominate the boys and the men of her acquaintance. To her, sex will become a symbol of *her* power and of *man's* vulnerability. She finds that with little effort she can make fools of men. In each conquest she will avenge herself upon the male as symbolized by her father. If she is clever, most men will be completely fooled by this mask of deceit. They will fall at her feet and do her bidding. She will find that her sexuality can be used to gain power, money and position, as well as revenge. In her heart she will secretly hate men. In her outward appearance and action she will give the impression of being seductive, warm or perhaps tender. She will respect no man, and her repeated conquests will seem to prove that no man deserves her respect. Perhaps inwardly she will always hope to find one man who can resist her tricks. Outwardly, she appears to want nothing more than to have a man at her feet. This revenge upon the male may take many forms. Whatever her methods or the pattern of her behavior, such a woman will go from one conquest to another, never satisfied until the man has submitted to her will. Each man will be a trophy added to her collection of conquests in her private battle of the sexes.

The mechanism will be much the same for a boy, who, for one reason or another, feels the need to revenge himself on a mother-image in which he has been disillusioned. He gives the outward appearance of being a great lover. In his mind he may consider that all women are trash. He is convinced that any woman upon whom he concentrates his attention will behave in an unvirtuous fashion. He loves none of them. He hates all of them. He may admit this feeling to himself, or he may conceal it from himself under elaborate alibis and rationalizations. He has never found love. He would scarcely recognize it if he did find it. He expects the worst of every woman. He goes from one woman to another continually proving to himself that his estimation of them is correct. If he is clever, he will develop a suave, smooth technique, by which he can subjugate the female. Women are toys to his whims. At the end of each conquest he may discard the woman or keep her on his "list" for an indefinite period to satisfy him as he wishes. In any case, each conquest is added to his collection.

When sex is thus used as a means of aggression, the years bring increasing feelings of frustration and dissatisfaction. The pursuit becomes less and less attractive, while higher and higher towers of virtue are assaulted in a never-ending cycle leading on to the inevitable self-disgust which always comes to those who have rated the opposite sex on a lower scale than themselves.

Sex Used as a Means of Reassurance and Security

Some individuals find sex can be used primarily as a means of gaining a synthetic love. They are basically insecure with a need to reassure themselves continually that they are attractive. They seek through sex the love which somehow they failed to receive in childhood. Sexual relationships, of one kind or another, bring a certain feeling of power over the environment. One who uses sex in this way has a constant need for proof of being a loved person.

Every individual has a normal need to feel that he is loved. If he fails to receive a sufficient amount of affection in early childhood, he may discover a substitute in sexual relationships, where a temporary feeling of security and of being wanted is possible. Sex then becomes a symbol of love received, rather than an expression of love shared. It is a grasping, seeking, urgent kind of sexuality. No sexual experience brings complete satisfaction under these conditions. The sense of insecurity remains unresolved—always pressing close to the surface of the mind. A vague feeling of incompleteness constantly threads its way into every day's activities, even when

69

events bring what should be appreciated as the best of circumstances. On the other hand, when things go wrong and difficulties arise in the day's happenings, the pressure of insecurity can become a torment of uncertainty. Sexual experiences are then desired as an antidote to futility.

In addition to sexual relationships with others, the insecure personality often finds himself caught in a pattern of compulsive masturbation. Through this practice uncertainties and fears are momentarily pushed into the background, only to return in more acute form at a later date. A more complete sexual satisfaction is then sought. New sensations, new relationships are canvassed in an attempt to find a synthetic substitute for the assurance of being loved.

The ego seeks through sexual experiences a reflection of itself. Because receiving, rather than sharing, is the real goal, rejection by intimates is a frequent occurrence. The seeking personality wishes to absorb and swallow up the whole life of sexual partners. The other individual begins to feel smothered in this demanding atmosphere. Eventually, that person resists the pressure to surrender his whole personality to the needs of his partner. Estrangement follows. Disillusionment, self-pity and strong feelings of insecurity again engulf the one who sought only to fulfill his emptiness in the relationship.

The real need is for the fulfillment of a picture of love similar to the idyllic love received by a little child in a so-called perfect home. People with this kind of pattern are always open for disillusionment because they are expecting the impossible in human relationship. They find it difficult to achieve any real love. They expect to be able to trade sexuality for love. This kind of need is without limit. It is a bottomless well. There is no satisfaction which can fill it. Each frustration and shattering of illusions only produces a greater need which, in turn, must be met in a more frantic attempt to purchase that which can only be given.

Sex Used for Satisfaction of Repressed Curiosity

Into this grouping we may place those who are primarily concerned with the biological process of sexuality. Their natural curiosity about sex was thwarted or repressed in early childhood, resulting in a morbid curiosity about the sex organs and their functions. The popularity of smutty stories among certain groups is motivated, in part, by repressed curiosity. Morbid curiosity about sex can ruin a marriage. There was the case of a young married couple whose problems began with an incident on their honeymoon. On the first night the young man shattered his bride's illusions of romance by insisting that he make a minute and curious inspection of her genital organs. It was quite evident to the bride that instead of a normal adult, she had married a young man who, at the moment, was primarily concerned with satisfying repressed childish curiosity. It seemed to her that this act was a denial of love. Her husband was more interested in her anatomy than he was in her as a person. This conclusion was borne out by later events. He seemed to lose interest in her sexually after his initial curiosity had been satisfied. To her further disgust, he became much more interested in looking at pictures of nude female figures than he was in any normal sexual relationship.

It is a sad commentary on our civilization that among primitive native tribes, where the human figure of both sexes is normally seen from childhood, this particular misuse of sexuality is not found.

Rebellion Expressed Through Sex

This is a problem peculiar to the adolescent. The big business of a child from about twelve or thirteen years of age until he is eighteen, is to become an adult independent of the authority of his parents. A great many parents make the serious mistake of attempting to cling to their children during these years. They feel that their children are not able to take care of themselves. Instead

71

of teaching adolescents to become independent and encouraging them in the art of making their own adult decisions, parents often dominate them under the false notion that they are being responsible parents.

Watch a parent bird when it is teaching young birds to fly. When the wings of the baby birds are fully formed, the parents begin to push the young out of the nest, thus encouraging them to test their wings in flight. The parents are always careful not to push a young bird out of the nest too rapidly, but the small one is encouraged to attempt flight *just a little sooner than he would normally try it himself.*

The job of a parent who has teen-age children is not too different than the bird's problem in teaching his young to fly. Human children, if they have any spirit at all, will assert their rights to be adults. Too many modern parents believe they are serving their children's best interests by providing an overly protective atmosphere. This is not love, it is possession. *The job of a parent is to become unnecessary to his children.* So common is the practice of parents clinging tightly to the control of their children that a great many well-educated American parents believe it is a normal part of development for their children to go through a period of rebellion. They fail to recognize that the child who must rebel against his parents in order to develop into an adult is a child who has not been permitted or encouraged to become an adult.

Since the teen age is the time in which dating usually begins and since a great many of the quarrels between teen-agers and their parents center around dating, sexual extravagance on the part of adolescents often becomes one of the symbols of rebellion.

The parents have said, "Sex is taboo. You *must* restrain yourself sexually until after marriage." The child who is seeking to rebel against parental authority at this age, can assert his independence by indulging in sexual behavior of which his parents disapprove.

It is not sex that the adolescent wants so much as he wants to prove to himself that he is an adult. Anything of which the parents strongly disapprove, and over which they attempt to exercise extreme control, becomes an object of rebellion when parents cling too tightly to the "apron strings." Daughters perhaps feel that if they are late coming home from a date, the father and mother will consider they have been spending their time in immoral fashion. They may feel that as long as they have the name, they might as well have the game. Boys in their teens, who are subjected to too strict parental controls, feel that their manhood is being called into question. These boys may discover that if they talk tough and act tough regarding sexual relationships, that the self-respect among their comrades will be restored.

Some adolescents carry this pattern of rebellion into adult life. For instance, there is the young man who marries young without having properly gone through a period of maturing. He finds in his bride only another symbol of responsibilities and controls that were placed upon him by his mother. Since he still has this need for rebellion, he adopts the practice of stepping out with other women. He may be perfectly satisfied sexually at home, but married life has brought an awareness that he has only exchanged the responsibilities and the restrictions of his parents for the responsibilities connected with being a husband. He likes to imagine that he is quite a man about town and that this independence is an expression of that manliness. Actually, he is still rebelling. He has not grown up and he continually needs to prove to himself through sex relationships that he is a man.

Any of the four misuses of sex which we have listed can produce a pattern of sexual behavior which psychologists call a compulsion. A compulsion expresses itself as an urge so demanding that in most cases it cannot be resisted by an effort of the will. When one has compulsive feelings, he may partially control them for a time. But when nothing is done to correct the cause of the compulsion, the individual will eventually yield to the urge, despite all efforts of will power.

Compulsions take many forms. Alcoholism is one kind of compulsive behavior. Compulsive patterns can also affect sex relationships. A sexual compulsion places a person in a peculiarly unhappy situation. It results, as a rule, in excessive sexual behavior which is strongly disapproved by society. The individual suffers from a fear that his peculiarity will be discovered. Enormous guilt feelings are sometimes felt because of the possibility of public exposure. As one becomes more acutely aware of the fact that he has no real control over this urge, he becomes desperate. Each time his behavior breaks over the boundaries of what he really wants to do, he vows to himself, "Never again." He makes promises for the future. He is certain that this time he will be able to control himself. But soon the compulsion returns and has its way, leaving him spent, guilt-ridden and terribly alone. He feels that no one can possibly understand his problem. He sometimes recognizes that he needs help, but he does not know where to turn. He wonders whether other people ever have this kind of difficulty. Sometimes, if his desperation becomes great enough, or if he has a depressive type of personality, he attempts suicide. There are times when he wallows in the quicksands of his own self-disgust and loathing. On other occasions, he feels a false sense of confidence and bolsters his feelings of insecurity by revelling in the fact that he can fly in the face of society's disapproval. Finally, he reaches the point where his own troubled emotions can only be laid to rest by yielding again to the compulsive urge. His compulsive activity brings less and less satisfaction and increasing misery. Yet, he is bound to it like a slave chained to a wheel. Ever increasing indulgence in his compulsive activity is necessary. There are times when he stops struggling against the compulsion and yields himself to it with abandon in the hope that his urges will be appeased. There are other times when he fights against the compulsion with all his will, attempting to change companions or to find some release in a new religion, a new philosophy or some regime of self-discpline.

He has been told that people who do the things which he does are lacking in will power and he thinks he must be a weakling. He does not know that will power cannot control his compulsion. Neither does he know that the compulsion is not his real problem, but only a symptom of inner emotional disturbances that must be resolved before the compulsive symptom will disappear.

Psychotherapy or very wise counseling is almost always necessary to find these deeper causes of compulsive behavior. Once the sources have been found, the individual can straighten out his life, provided he wants to revise his thinking about all things. No one is really capable of changing his basic patterns of feeling unless he wants this change more than anything else in the world and, even then, outside aid is usually necessary.

Those who have not suffered from compulsive behavior cannot understand the agony or the helplessness suffered by those individuals caught in the clutches of such a symptom. Those unafflicted with this problem will say that normal living is simply a matter of will power. They do not know how often the individual suffering from a compulsion has told himself the same thing. Compulsive behavior hits the strong and the weak, the rich and the poor, the educated and the uneducated. It is no respecter of persons.

Compulsive sexual behavior is often accompanied by elaborate sexual fantasies. This is not true in every case, but for those whose compulsions are connected with highly imaginative fantasies, the emotional problems are more complex.

Everyone has day dreams, everyone has a world of imagination in which he spends part of his time. Fantasy becomes unwholesome only when it serves as a substitute for reality. Someone has said that the mark of a genius is the ability to drop the cares and responsibilities of an adult world for a period of childish play. To be able to find brief relaxation in play is one of the marks of the disciplined mind. The individual who is incapable of exercising imagination or of being playfully informal is a particularly rigid kind of personality. The inability to let loose and play, the constant need to be serious and dignified, can be as damaging a compulsion as any of those that we have been describing. This sort of rigidity is frequently only a reverse aspect of distorted sexuality. It displays an inability to be honest with one's self.

Play and relaxation are a normal function for any mature personality. Day dreams are the stuff of the play world. Like all good things, however, imagination can become distorted or misused. When the world of make-believe becomes more important than the world of reality, the individual is in trouble. When happiness or satisfaction is sought through the continual reliving of certain fantasies, a person is not only prevented from coping adequately with his environment, but also finds his real world twisted out of shape by the fantasies of a day-dream world. The sportsman who stands on the bank of a crystal-clear mountain stream and attempts to spear fish below the surface quickly learns to compensate for the distortion of light rays as they enter the water. The individual who lives in the depths of his fantasy world is usually not so fortunate. As he attempts to strike at the objectives of his desires in the real world, his efforts go wide of the mark. Reality is distorted as his thoughts enter the world of fantasy. Increasingly, he is unable to distinguish where reality ends and fantasy begins.

In the case of sexual fantasies, the distortion of inner vision is further accented by the hidden guilt feelings that accompany his fantasy life. His day-dreams usually take the form of the forbidden, or of that which is socially disapproved. Thus, he must build ever-increasing vividness of fantasy and greater elaboration of details in order to hide from himself the fact that he is poorly adjusted or unhappy with reality.

To break the spell of the world of fantasy, one must first recognize that too much self-blame should not be attached to his preoccupation with the world of imagination. The alternative to creating a world of fantasy is, for some individuals, complete insanity. Fantasy is the only protection against the too bright glare of reality.

The fantasy world usually develops during childhood. To the child in an unhappy home, the inner world of daydreams may be the only practical outlet. However, when one continues at the adult age to indulge in a great amount of such daydreaming, he is following a practice no longer necessary to him. In a mild form we can see an example in observing little children at play. Frequently, they will talk to themselves or to an imaginary companion. In a child this is considered to be quite normal. In an adult, who can supposedly control his environment to some extent, it becomes ridiculous.

As we have just indicated, when compulsive sexual behavior is strengthened by daydreams it becomes a perfect temporary escape from the realities of the present. Addiction to this pattern will sometimes have a stronger hold upon the individual than alcoholism. Whenever a person is threatened or fearful, he will return to the old daydreams and the old compulsions. He does not know how to free himself from the trap until he learns, perhaps through the aid of a psychiatrist, new and better ways for securing satisfaction in reality. As long as the fantasy world continues to be predominant, a person will continue to be strongly dissatisfied with any of the circumstances in which he finds himself. By simply flipping a mental switch, he can construct a far more satisfactory world than seems possible to him in the real world.

For instance, a lady client is married to a man who is no better or worse than many husbands. He is dependable, devoted and, under ordinary circumstances, would be a good husband. Since childhood this woman has constructed an elaborate fantasy of a handsome, wealthy, glamorous man who comes into her daydream, sweeps her off her feet, marries her and deposits her in a beautiful mansion of leisure and excitement. Whenever the duties of the home or the problems of finances press upon her, as they do upon all of us, she takes to her bed, gives herself a mild sedative and retreats into her dream world. This only adds to her dissatisfaction with her husband, her irritation at the children. She hates herself while she is doing this, but finds such great satisfaction in the retreat that even though she has reached middle age, she has not been able to give up the practice. During such periods of escape her average husband seems like a clod, her normal children becomes brats, her house seems like a hovel and depression settles upon her. With her dream prince she can flee from all of this, while she lives for a time in her world of make-believe.

Then there is the husband who is married to a frigid wife. She might not be frigid if he were more adept at living in the real world. But he needs to imagine that he is married to a sexually demanding and passionate woman. He is a man of strict morals who cannot bring himself to have an affair with another woman, even though this is something which he desires. Perhaps it is only fear of social consequences, rather than conscience, which prevents him from doing that which he wishes. In any case, he remains outwardly true to his wife while he constructs a dream world in which he is ardently wooed by a beautiful woman. Thus, he escapes from a problem he does not wish to face fully. By the very escape he places himself in a position where he is less able to discover married happiness with the woman of his early choice.

The illusions of fantasy are without number. They are as varied as the individuals who entertain them. Each constructs the kind of dream that will give him the greatest satisfaction, retreating ever further from the possibility of founding a solid happiness upon fact.

Many frustrated people lead what has been called the "life of quiet desperation." Others live exceedingly exciting lives in the world fantasy. In this world, the extent of the retreat from life is only limited by the individual's power of imagination. Man needs his dreams, but as Kipling pointed out, one of the marks of the man is the ability to "dream and not make dreams your master."

Because of the strong social disapproval connected with all unusual sexual behavior, the individual suffering from a sexual compulsion can often wreck his career or his life if his irregularities are publicly known.

Society has come to recognize that alcoholism is an illness, but the anonimity of Alcoholics Anonymous is still a most necessary safeguard for those who would reconstruct their lives from the wreckage of the past.

There will come a time when society will likewise recognize that those who suffer from sexual compulsions are emotionally ill. Until such a time, the informal society of those who have helped one another to recover from this problem will by necessity have to remain anonymous. Like those with a compulsion to drink, individuals suffering from sexual compulsions have usually found very little help through organized religion or conventional psychiatric methods. For everyone who finds recovery through these avenues there are ten others who do not find relief. They either do not know that the problem is an illness or they have no notion of where to seek help. Many of them have not yet come to a realization that they truly need assistance.

In the following chapter we shall attempt to offer some concrete suggestions for those who wish to remove the sexual mask of deceit from their lives.

Chapter VIII

A Step Beyond Understanding

Few people can honestly say that they have been without some sexual problems. The great majority of the population will experience difficulties of one sort or another between childhood and old age. Fortunately, most of these individuals may not find sex any more of a problem than numerous other responsibilities demanded of adults. Short periods of adjustment will bring satisfactory solutions to most of their difficulties.

However, another group of people exists for whom sex is the major problem of life. Some of them will be unwilling to admit it, even to themselves. Others will make the admission but will, as yet, be uninformed about how to escape from the trap of their particular kind of emotional cage.

These individuals, for whom sex is a major threat to peace of mind, are as different from ordinary folk as the alcoholic is different from the social drinker. They are different because they suffer from what we call compulsive behavior, over which they often have little or no control by mere will power. Sexual and alcoholic compulsions have much in common. The alcoholic can free himself of his compulsion by establishing a new pattern of thinking, by developing a new set of responses to his environment and by then refraining from taking the first drink. Even after years of sobriety, if he returns to the pattern of the first drink, he slips easily back into the old alcoholic way of life. In order for the alcoholic to take the first drink, his thinking must first have reverted to some of the old undesirable pattern. He must have begun to develop elaborate alibis and rationalizations. Then, when he does drink, he continues at an accelerated rate along the course of his emotional "bender."

Finally, remorse comes to him. He is full of self-disgust because he has broken faith with himself. He remembers that he forsook a better way of life to plunge himself into this hell of fear, guilt and self-accusation. In many cases, especially if understanding help is available, he will climb back out of his morass before the swamp of despair closes over his head. He will then be a better person through the lessons he has learned from his relapse.

The sexual compulsive finds himself in a very similar position. Control of his compulsive pressures is only possible through (1) a high degree of understanding about the inner conflicts which have found a compensation through sex and (2) an earnest attempt to rebuild a way of thinking around the nucleus of these new insights.

If a relapse occurs, it is always preceded by a partial return to old patterns of thinking. The individual will believe he is being most reasonable when, in reality, his thinking about sex will be dominated by elaborate alibis and rationalizations. If he can recognize this fact well enough to delay a return to old patterns of action until he can correct his thinking, he will save himself much trouble. If not, he will proceed toward the old pattern with no will or ability to halt the process.

Like the alcoholic, he has a good chance of a return to normal thinking if he has adequate help. In the case of either alcoholic or sexual compulsions, recovery is dependent first upon an earnest desire for serenity and, second, upon a willingness to recognize that without serenity one's life will be unmanageable.

The difference between ordinary sexual behavior and the sexual behavior displayed by the compulsive personality is not easily determined. Often, there is little apparent difference in the acts of the two groups. *The distinction between normal and compulsive sexual behavior is best known to the individual involved.* Compulsive sexuality is distinguished by the relationship of certain repeated patterns of behavior. Unfortunately, these patterns are not too well defined. Very little exact research has been done on the progressive development of sexual compulsions. Mental preoccupation with sex and sex objects, elaborate sexual fantasies, casual affairs and the development of alibis for indulgence are some of the symptoms.

People with normal emotional reactions toward sex may, upon occasion, find themselves in a sexual situation which is damaging to health, position or a valued home. Confronted with the choice between the pleasure of a moment and permanent injury to an important part of their lives, they will resolve never again to become so involved. They will be able to carry out their firm resolutions.

Those who suffer from sexual compulsions, on the other hand, are faced with quite a different kind of problem. In a sexual situation that threatens some major part of their lives, they will extricate themselves and make a resolve that never again will they become so involved. However, this resolution will only be temporary. They will soon find themselves repeating the old pattern of behavior. *They will not keep their resolutions.*

The emotional problem of a compulsive personality functions the same, whether it involves alcohol or sex. Will power —the desire to change—is needed to find serenity. But will power, without help and without understanding, is inadequate every time it is tried. *If one can solve the problem with will power alone, he was not suffering from a compulsion.* This is the ultimate and final distinguishing line which separates ordinary sexual excesses from compulsive sexuality.

The first step in freeing one's self from a compulsion is to admit that it exists—that its presence is an uncontrollable factor in one's life. Those with sexual compulsions must come to a realization that the ordinary methods of control will not work, that there is something basically wrong with the self, which makes this area of life unmanageable.

Most people with serious compulsions have gone through periods when they have used the compelling nature of their desires as an excuse for unrestrained indulgence. They have said, "This thing seems uncontrolable, I might as well yield myself to it." In this mood it is easy to say, "Why make the effort to resist?"

Therefore, when one takes the first step toward recovery by admitting the seriousness of sexual compulsions, he is actually saying, "This compulsion is evidence that my whole way of life is unmanageable." Along with this admission must come a growing understanding of *why* one's particular personality needs to maintain the compulsion as a balance wheel.

The compulsion toward certain kinds of sexual behavior is not the *real* problem, any more than alcohol is the basic problem of the alcoholic. True, compulsions may produce such serious effects that they overshadow the original cause. But the primary problem of the alcoholic is in his mind, not in the bottle. The problem of the sexually compulsive personality is in his mind, not in his glands.

A compulsion, however painful its effects may be at times, is only a symptom of a deeper illness. Fortunately, through psychotherapy and various group therapies we now have tools for discovering these deeper causes within ourselves. We are then able to correct the cause and find ourselves liberated from the painful symptoms. We can at last be free of compulsive behavior which threatens to drive us toward a destiny we did not choose.

Even after we have found the answers to the personality conflicts within ourselves and have taken steps to correct them, old habits of thought have a subtle way of sneaking back upon us. When this happens the compulsive feelings are apt to reassert themselves.

How can we guard against these threats before damage is done which is difficult to repair?

We have called this chapter "A Step Beyond Understanding." Freedom and a new sense of inner serenity have come to us through understanding our sexual motivations. What are some of the practical things we can now do to step beyond understanding into the everyday application of our new knowledge?

Everyone must use those methods which work best for him. For no two people are the problems exactly the same. The solutions, also, must be tailored to fit one's own needs. Each has his own strength, his own weakness, his own brand of "stinking thinking," against which he must learn to safeguard his mind. Fear and defeat can come to all men. They do not come to all men in the same way. Serenity and successful living can also come to all who will search. But they will be found by each man a little differently than for every other man. The suggestions we offer here are clues gained from the experience of those who have found methods for maintaining their sexual equilibrium.

First, try to cultivate at least one close friend who has a problem similar to your own, someone in whom you have the deepest trust, someone with whom you can share thoughts and feelings, someone who knows you well enough to alert you to danger when your thinking is becoming twisted.

If you are close enough to your psychiatrist or if you are wealthy enough to afford his continued services, you will go to him. Most of us are not that fortunate. A friend will do—if he has a problem similar to your own, *and is sincerely trying to do something about it.*

Second, when a compulsive urge returns, be prepared to reject its first demand for action. If the alcoholic does not take the first drink, he will not get drunk. The first yielding to a sexual compulsion is the one which leads to further yielding.

Do anything—anything which will momentarily distract your attention from sex. *But do not yield to this first compulsive urge.* Remember, it is always the first act which starts you on a series of acts.

Third, call your friend and get to him at the first available opportunity. He will understand your need to talk and will clear his schedule. He can help you find where your thinking became muddled in the first place. He will give you the support, the confidence and, most of all, the permissive understanding you need to cope with your problem.

Get to your friend *before* you slip. However, if your compulsion did get out of hand before you had presence of mind or the will to stop, go to your friend as soon as possible and get his help before matters become worse.

Fourth, take care to distinguish between normal sexual desire and sexual compulsion. In denying the compulsion, do not deny your own human nature. For instance, masturbation for either sex can be a driving compulsive activity which brings little release and is followed by enormous feelings of guilt. Or, it can be a useful means of releasing sexual tension when other normal outlets are not possible or proper.

The need for sexual outlet varies widely between individuals. One member of a marriage may find that married happiness will be improved if he has some supplementary sex outlet. If the spouse is properly understanding, he or she will help to provide this additional outlet by forms of sexual play, other than intercourse. There may be circumstances where masturbation can be of some real help.

It should always be kept in mind, however, that these are supplements. They are not substitutes for the complete sexual relationship which exists between a man and woman who love one another.

Those who have suffered from sexual compulsions are usually people who have seldom, if ever, discovered what they consider to be the complete fulfillment of love in a sexual relationship. They may be in such a situation that they will never experience it. Nevertheless, if they are to maintain peace of mind, they must stop seeking in variety that which they have not found in one relationship.

Because fantasy has played a large part in their compulsive pattern, they have often constructed an imaginary picture of complete sexual fulfillment. It is this imaginary picture which sometimes drives the compulsive personality toward a succession of affairs—always seeking and never finding, looking for sexual perfection in the self-centered pattern of his own fantasies.

This pattern is a delusion and a snare. It tends to negate the element of sharing in love and exaggerates the element of sex in adjustment of the sexes.

Fifth, it is important to know that the essence of true sexual fulfillment is in the *quality* of the experience, *not* in the *quantity*. No amount of quantity can ever produce the fulfillment to be found in quality. Sexual compulsions drive one toward a pattern that seeks in quantity that which has not been found in quality. Only frustration lies along this route, for the continual search after quantity eventually makes it impossible to experience quality.

The quality of sexual relationship is dependent upon the love that is expressed and shared by a man and a woman. It is a blending of all that represents the mature intelligence, emotions and physique.

Sixth, in establishing new patterns that will reduce the risk of recurring sexual compulsions, one should endeavor to improve all sexual attitudes. If one is married, time may have brought serious problems of impotence or frigidity. A positive attempt to meet these problems will bring rewards that will help to remove many conflicts which trigger the explosive forces of compulsion.

If one has spent time and money with a psychiatrist, he should get the most from the investment by renewing active courtship of the wife or husband, as the case may be, after the renovating therapy of the psychiatrist. If a man has been a Don Juan before therapy, he is missing a real opportunity to further his mental health when he fails to become reacquainted with his wife.

Sexual compulsions are not removed by resigning from the world of sex. They only disappear gradually, as one increasingly develops a realignment of basic needs and basic ways of satisfying these needs.

Seventh, the best antidote for sexual compulsion, or any other symptom of emotional imbalance, is the preservation of correct thinking and action in all areas of life. Since the compulsion is always a symptom, rather than a basic cause of emotional immaturity, it will only reappear at those times when incorrect thinking has again crept into the mind. Return of the compulsive feeling is an indication that something is wrong below the immediate conscious level of the mind. Old fears, old anxieties, old guilt feelings are reasserting themselves.

Look quickly, then, to the causes! Seek out the incident which has again brought these forces into renewed action. Do not be put off by excuses. Seek the causes. They will certainly be found to lie in the areas where the pressure points of former immaturities had previously produced emotional breakdown. It is folly to suppose that a period of emotional stability renders one immune to the recurrence of old irrational thinking.

Find the emotional "monkey-wrench" that is clogging the mental machinery. Remove this impediment once more by recognizing its nature. Immediately the sense of peace—the inner certainty of correct relaxed thinking —will begin to return. The compulsive symptom will disappear also. The mind will again be at home with itself.

You will experience that wonderfully liberating feeling of inner serenity!

Chapter IX

Living One Day at a Time

Today is the only day in which you can live. Tomorrow you may be dead. Yesterday, with all its mistakes and all its pleasures, is gone forever. Today is here with its promise of what you make it. Today you may feel you are in a terrible situation, but by your efforts you can make the present a little better if you will stop living in the past and the future. Whether the quality of the present seems good or bad, it is the only time you have.

The present moment is infinitely precious. If you have a boy who is grown and has left home, you have looked at a picture of him taken when he was a laughing lad of ten or twelve years. All the memories of those early years have returned to your mind. Perhaps you have wished for a moment that he was young again and you had him with you at home. Those early years passed so quickly. You enjoyed good times with him, but you would like to have had more of them.

At such a moment of remembrance you realize how every day passes too quickly. You may wish you had taken more time to be with your boy when he was home. You know that the past can only be remembered with pleasure if the present is lived to its fullest. You know the futility of anxiety about the future or regret for the unchanging past.

The present holds the seeds of eternity. In the split second of the present you are aware of yourself and of your world. If you are at home with yourself, the present moment offers an opportunity for a little touch of heaven. If you are not at home with yourself, this moment can bring you a small awareness of torture which we can only describe as hell.

Even though you know how precious is the present, you sometimes weave the threads of tragedy into your life by the persistent habit of spending more time living in the past and the future than in the present.

The simplicity of little children can teach a great lesson. Watch a child at play. He stumbles and falls. He cries. Mother picks him up and comforts his hurt. In a moment he is running and laughing again. The pain of the past moment is soon forgotten in the pleasures of his play. In our anxiety for the future and the pressure of past mistakes we adults forget this art. We forget that this moment is all we have. We forget how to live today. Perhaps we come to believe that today will be as bad as yesterday and tomorrow may be worse. We have lost our faith in today. We have lost our belief in our own capacity to improve anything.

You, and you alone, have the power to try making something worthwhile of today. Living brings pain to all of us in time. Living brings its moments of desperation, its hours when nothing seems to go right and hope is lost in the darkness. Physical disability can bring its pain, mental problems can bring their agony, one's own acts can inflict their disgrace. There is no end to the catalogue of human disaster. No man or woman is immune. But observe the man with much peace in his soul. He will be a man upon whom life has inflicted many scars. He will be a man who has learned some ability to live one day at a time.

You may be one of those who have escaped from the pain of the present by pursuing the future with hectic activity. Outwardly you may appear to be living a full life. You have engaged in an endless round of hurry. Inwardly your frenzied activity in the present has been directed entirely toward the goal of the future. You have been so busy living for tomorrow that there is no sense of inner calm in the present. You have excused your total preoccupation with the future by calling it "realistic planning."

Some people escape the present in a different way. They

89

rob the present of its greatest reward by living in the reminiscences of the vain regrets of yesterday. Like the Wahoo Bird, they fly backwards so that they will have an unobstructed view of where they have been.

Preoccupation with the past and the future will not kill the pain of the present. The only real solution is to pause, look deeply within one's self, face today's problems with rigorous self-honesty and make what choices the day demands.

The burdens of the tomorrows and the yesterdays are too great for any individual to bear. If one thinks of his life in terms of all the things that he must do tomorrow, next week or next year, the sheer weight of the resulting worry is enough to fatigue the strongest frame. Many people seek a synthetic security by attempting to plan their lives in detail for a year in advance. Planning is a healthy, normal function of the human mind. We must all plan. But when planning for the future distracts us from today, it becomes an intolerable burden.

Preoccupation with the future is a damaging habit in several ways. First, it fills the mind with fruitless speculation, leaving no room for concentration on the present. Concern with the problem of how to cross the glacier of tomorrow blinds us to the little stones at our feet. It is the little daily problems which cause us to trip and fall. Most of us do quite well when we are actually confronted with an occasional big problem. It is the accumulation of little problems which confound us.

Second, we fail to appreciate the valuable and happy experiences at hand when our minds are not upon the present. We are so concerned with the problem of how to pay tomorrow's debt that we miss seeing today's sunset. We often worry so much about how to pay for our children's education that we do not enjoy their pleasant childish laughter. Thus, we fail to see or hear or feel the wonderful things which are around us today.

Third, on the basis of today's experiences, we can only anticipate the *problems* of tomorrow. We are incapable of visualizing the *good* things which will happen to us in the future. The inability of the human mind to foresee the good events of tomorrow is clearly illustrated in the prophetic writing of the Old Testament, with which most of us are familiar. These prophetic writers were wise men but, like all of us, their predictions were mostly concerned with doom. On the basis of the confused present, they could predict the disasters of tomorrow. They were unable to visualize the good and creative events which history later proved the universe could provide.

Most of us know that worry is futile, but how can we stop worrying? We tell ourselves and our friends, "Don't worry about it. It will work out all right." We have learned that it is useless to say to one's self, "I will not worry." This is a negative approach. Worry cannot be turned off like a water faucet. As long as a human being is alive and conscious, he is going to think. The only way to solve this problem is to fill the mind so full of thoughts about the present that there remains no space for negative thoughts about the future. The answer is not to stop thinking or to stop worrying, but to redirect the thought into a new channel.

The present moment is large enough and interesting enough to occupy all our attention if we will but learn to focus our thoughts upon it. Those who have learned to think and to live in this manner find the present is an ever-expanding moment into which all their energies and thoughts can flow.

It is a beautiful thing to see the change of thinking which comes over a rehabilitated alcoholic when he stops demeaning the present with alcohol and suddenly becomes aware of the life around him. He is like a child who wakens from a dreamless sleep to find a beautiful day lying fresh before him with all its wonderful beauty and opportunities. In this mood he experiences the simple joy of being alive. As long as he continues to think and to act in the present he is a happy man who is released from his tensions. The moment he drops into the old pattern of anxiety about the future, his joy deserts him and his sobriety disappears along with it.

Jesus once said, "No man can serve two masters." He understood that singlemindedness is the price we must pay for a well adjusted personality. We could paraphrase this statement and say, "No man can serve yesterday, today and tomorrow." In living abundantly in the present moment, we find our real selves. Man is the only living creature with foresight and hindsight. He can use these gifts to lead a full life, but it should be a full life in the present if the past and the future are to have a vitality and meaning.

Thomas Wolfe once said, "You can't go home again." In this phrase he summed up the problem of those who are forever looking backwards, seeking to return to some moment of childish paradise where escape from the responsibilities of the present could be found. The individual who lives in the past is just as confused as the person who devotes his time to the future. It makes no difference whether he looks upon the past with regret or with longing. In either case he is distracted from the business at hand. Yesterday is gone. It may have brought happiness or despair, but it is gone. He can no longer live in it. There is no virtue in directing one's concentration on yesterday.

Every clergyman is well familiar with the figure of the individual who has lost some loved person by death, only to spend years looking backward with regret or happiness to the past. The past is only good for two things; to give pleasure to the present or to teach lessons for the present. An occasional backward glance is a good thing. After that glance, one should turn again with a smile to the path of the present, plant his feet firmly on today's trail and climb the steps in today's stair. Each individual, when he wakens in the morning, should say to himself, "This is my day to spend. This day I will be the best person I am capable of being. I will face today with expectancy, anticipating that some of the things which the day brings will be good and some of the experiences will be bad."

One should begin the day with a thought of thanks for the opportunity of living. Then, when the day is done and he lies down again to rest, he should review the day briefly in his mind and ask himself, "What did I do right and what did I do wrong? Are there any lessons which this day taught me?" Each day will bring its lesson and each day will bring its own satisfaction. Having distilled from the day's experiences the lessons which it brought, he should be thankful. He should say to himself, "If tomorrow comes, I will use the lessons of today as the opportunity is presented." He should not carry his regrets, his resentments or his frustrations into a period of sleep. The individual who thus learns to live one day at a time will discover to his amazement that after a year or two years, he can look back upon a better life—one in which many good things have occurred to him.

Not long ago, the author was attending an Alcoholics Anonymous meeting. A young man, who had been sober for a period of several months, was describing his experiences at the first AA meeting he ever attended. He had been impressed by the talk of an older member, who stated he had been sober continuously for over five years. The older member went on to say that he might be drunk tomorrow, but today he was sober. In commenting on this talk, the new member of the group stated that at the time he thought the older man must be "touched in the head" to make such a statement. After all, he had been sober for five years and he should be able to say with some assurance that he would be sober next year. But the young alcoholic said that he soon learned this was the only satisfactory way that anyone could live—one day at a time. Promises made to the future are no good. The only promises that have strength and vitality are promises made to the present.

It would seem that any of us ought to have enough common sense to understand that today is our task; yet we flounder through life regretful of the past, frustrated about the present and desperate about the future, because we are trying to live in all three areas at once.

No one has expressed this thought better than Jesus when He said, "Sufficient unto the day is the evil thereof." He well understood that the present is the Eternal Now. In this present moment we touch a small inlet of the greater sea of our eternity. Whether this inlet is a portion of heaven or hell depends on our own thinking as we live today.

Kagawa, the great Japanese thinker, on one occasion found himself in a solitary prison cell where he had been placed by his fellow citizens because of his opposition to the militaristic attitude before Pearl Harbor. The cell was scarcely large enough for him to lie down and the only window was a small barred aperture close to the ceiling far above his head. One night he was standing in his cell where he could see a small star shining through the bars of this tiny window. Alone, rejected, ill from poor food, Kagawa wrote a poem about that star. In its light he felt at that moment a contact with all mankind and with all the universe, and he was glad in his heart because it still shone for him in a darkened cell. The future held no hope, the past seemed futile, the present was not promising, but in concentrating upon this moment of beauty, he found contact with the Eternal Now.

Trouble may be all around us; sickness, death and despair may seem to be our lot; but for each of us in this moment there is something for which life is worth living. We will find it if we concentrate upon the present.

Self-pity, inner dishonesty, resentment and anxiety are foes of these moments of appreciation, but enjoyment of life can come to us if we will look for it.

If we imagine that we must grasp all of life around us, feeling that we can command past, present and future to do our bidding, we are attempting to take to ourselves too large an area. No man can command this much territory. When we live beyond the present we are living beyond our means. We are attempting to do something which is impossible. We must turn within ourselves and learn that our bigness will be found in the small moment of the present. Our usefulness will be expressed in the service we can give *now*.

Time is only a yardstick of memory and anticipation. Time is a very small thing. Eternity is huge. It can be found for each of us in the present.

Chapter X

Why Don't They Get Well?

Those who work with the emotionally disturbed tend to develop a philosophical attitude about that percentage of individuals who make a start toward maturity, only to slip back into the old patterns. Like the physician, they soon learn to realize that a certain percentage will get well, while others will die of their illnesses. This does not make them less sensitive to the tragedy of failure. Often they ponder the reasons why some promising individual failed to continue his growth. There are no pat answers to this question. In the case of emotional disturbance there are no quick solutions or easy panaceas which will produce a miracle by taking a pill.

People of the future will undoubtedly look back with amusement upon our feeble attempts to help the emotionally disturbed. Perhaps in the future we shall discover ways to produce a society in which little children will develop better emotional patterns to equip them for adult life.

In spite of our limited knowledge, there are some reasons for failure that are quite clear to us. It might be well to suggest some of the more common ones.

A great many people fail to achieve emotional maturity as adults because they have never learned to distinguish between respectability and sanity. Or, to put it another way, respectability is more important to them than sanity. They fail to realize that true sanity will produce its own respectability. A good example of this peculiar twist in the thinking of some people is often seen in alcoholics when they first start to attend Alcoholics Anonymous meetings. During their drinking days, they were under the delusion that families and acquaintances were unaware that they had a problem. For years they fooled themselves so well that they imagined the neighbors had noticed nothing peculiar. It is hard to imagine how far this self-deception can go. An alcoholic can have a battle with his wife, during which they scream at each other and at the children. Furniture may be broken. The police may be called to quiet the disturbance. Yet the alcoholic never seems to realize that a good deal of this is apparent to the neighbors. Naturally, he is in such a deep alcoholic fog much of the time that he is unaware of the world around him. He likewise imagines that the world is unaware of him and his behavior. He may be irritable and unreasonable at work. He may develop antisocial behavior. He can insult his friends, borrow money from his relatives without paying it back, let the household bills accumulate and drive erratically down the highway from one side to another, yet he thinks that very few people observe this, simply because he is careful to chew great quantities of chlorophyl gum and sprinkle his person profusely with shaving lotion.

Finally, he comes to the end of his rope, decides he has a problem, and makes a tentative approach to a member of Alcoholics Anonymous. When he is invited to attend his first meeting, he suddenly develops a great self-consciousness about his problem. He sometimes refuses to accept help because he feels that now everyone will know that he is an alcoholic. It often takes considerable persuading to convince him that everyone has known for a long time that he was an alcoholic. He, alone, was oblivious to his problem.

If a man continually behaves in an objectionable fashion there is no point in trying to cover it up. Everyone usually knows there is something wrong a long time before he is willing to admit it. What respectability he may have possessed at one time was lost long ago. Still, he imagines that people associate with him because they like him when, in reality, they only associate with him because they cannot avoid him. An individual in this position, who insists on clinging to the tattered threads of his respectability, will not get well. *He will not get well because he has really not accepted the fact that he is sick.* Naked and alone, exposed to the winds of social disapproval, he cannot clothe himself in the garments of sanity until he is willing to recognize his own nakedness, honestly face the shame of the past and seek a new set of clothes, wherever they can be found.

Every individual who has ever been released from a mental hospital knows that upsurge of fear which comes at the prospect of facing his associates in the community. Like the trapeze artist who has slipped from the wire and suffered serious injury, his self-respect and social courage can only be restored by climbing again boldly to the high wire and conquering his fear. He will be helped in this if he realizes that he has joined the vast company of those whose successes have been built upon failures.

When we are faced with this adjustment to society, we must decide whether it is social approval or sanity which we wish. It does no good for us to say to ourselves we care not what others think. We care a great deal for the good opinion of our acquaintances, but most of us imagine we are held in higher regard by our acquaintances than we are.

Part of this problem is created by a general attitude of society. For most of us, respectability is part of our economic structure of trade. Our society exacts a far higher penalty upon those who are not considered respectable than it does upon those whose emotions may be immature. The idea that we can do as we please, as long as we do not get caught, is widely accepted by a great number of people in society.

These attitudes carry over to those whose problems are emotional. If one suffers a nervous breakdown or discovers he is an alcoholic, it is helpful to realize that mental illness is now the largest public health problem in the nation. This means that within one's immediate neighborhood there are usually several people who, through personal experiences, are sympathetic toward these problems. Also it is encouraging to know that some of our most outstanding citizens are numbered among those who sought and found help from mental disturbance to mental health.

Many people, who are supposedly well-educated, find it necessary to build their own egos by a self-righteous pride in the fact that they have been able to manage their own lives without ever becoming emotionally ill. Some of these are mature enough to recognize that what has happened to others might well happen to them, but there are many who like to imagine they are mature and sane in every way because they are respectable. They attribute mental illness to a failure of the will, to some moral fault, or some weakness of character. They do not recognize that it is often the perfectionist, the man of stubborn pride, or the woman of superior imagination who cracks under the pressures of daily living. Perhaps they fail to see in themselves the little quirks and compulsions—minor immaturities—which make it difficult for others to live with them. At the same time they condemn those whose compulsive behavior happens to be of a kind that is socially unacceptable.

Often the man who clings stubbornly to a certain point of view long after he has been proven wrong, suffers from as tenacious a compulsion as any alcoholic. The husband who practices sadistic mental torture upon his family is mentally as far off base as the Wild Beast of Buchenwald Prison. His crime is only one of lesser degree; his emotional immaturity is only tolerated because it is practiced out of the eye of the public. The individual whose humor is primarily concerned with smutty and unfunny stories is just as much a sexual exhibitionist as the mental case who cannot resist the compulsion to expose his body to the opposite sex in public.

It is high time that we stripped the mask from these little perversions of the mind that prevent us from seeing ourselves as we are seen. It can almost be said without exception that the individual who is smug in his own strength has no justification for feeling superior to those whose emotional immaturities are more obvious.

The individual who needs to recover his own sanity must achieve enough emotional maturity to recognize that the sneers of such people are products of immature minds. He will only achieve such an objective when he learns that his own sanity, his own inner peace of mind, is far more important than gaining universal approval. If we must wait for our sanity until everyone accepts us and treats us with understanding, we will never become sane.

There is another kind of problem which prevents many people from finding the goal of their inner serenity. These are the ones who continually seek what has been called "the geographical cure." They have never quite been able to accept the fact that their problems lie within themselves. The "geographical cure" can take the form of a new job, a new location, a new family or perhaps a new fad. Always the pasture looks greener on the other side of the fence. Those who seek to solve emotional problems by an external change often admit their difficulties are partly caused by inner tension, but they blame external conditions for most of the trouble.

It is certainly true that many people can and do find their solution in a new situation. It is quite possible that a man may be working at a job for which he is not fitted. If he has the courage or the spirit to seek a different employment, many of his conflicts and tensions might disappear. But aimlessly seeking the same kind of a job in a different location is not the answer to inner pressure.

We have all seen the futile struggle of those whose lives are a continuous history of going from one job to another, or from one town to another, always finding themselves eventually faced with the same problem as confronted them in the last location. The only solution is to stop and face reality with a willingness to recognize the internal nature of the problem. As long as one considers his whole problem to be external, he will make no effort toward self-improvement.

Some years ago, a young man came to me for counseling with a personal problem. He realized that his emotional attitudes were producing a severe and chronic discontent. After several interviews, he came to understand that many of his pressures became noticeable at the time he was in the armed forces during World War II. While he was in the service, his fiance married another man. When the client returned from the war, he found himself unable to forget the girl and could not make a satisfactory adjustment to civilian life. He had tried dating a number of other women, but did not become seriously interested in any of them because of the emotional turmoil within himself. At the same time, he wanted very much to find a young woman with whom he could fall in love and make a home. He kept insisting that if he could find the right girl, all of his immaturities would disappear. I attempted to lead him toward a realization that until he had faced his own emotional conflicts, he could not expect to make a satisfactory marriage, even if he found what he considered the right girl. After several more counseling sessions, he terminated the interviews. About a year later he thought that he had met the right girl. They were married. The marriage soon ended in divorce and the young man found himself in even worse emotional condition than before. So far as I know, this man, who is now middle aged, is still running away from his problems.

There are a great many persons who are caught in this particular kind of frustrating pattern. When they find themselves in deep enough trouble they seek a little help. When they discover that the solutions to their problems demand a *radical change* within their own personalities, they begin to dodge the issue. Their failure to make a good recovery results from an apparent unwillingness to admit the extent of their own emotional illness. To admit that ninety per cent of their problems is internal seems to threaten their inner security to such an extent that they are unable to face fully the facts about themselves. In seeking counseling or psychotherapy, they make what appears to be a very promising start, only to drop the whole thing after the going gets rough. If they have money enough to afford it, they go from one psychiatrist to another and when they run out of psychiatrists they are apt to be found pursuing some new religious fad or some new avocation about which they have become temporarily very enthusiastic. Their behavior is the despair of their families, since their recurrent crises are usually expensive and their techniques for gaining sympathy are highly developed. They are not able to maintain long-standing friendships, because they ride every new friendship to death in the same way that they consume their new fads and interests.

They launch into any new project with immense enthusiasm, which quickly turns into resentment and dissatisfaction as they fail to receive the satisfaction which they seek. Each new location, each new job or interest is soon dropped for what appears to be a more promising prospect.

There was a man of my acquaintance who exhibited this pattern in a form of a series of hobbies. He filled his garage with the equipment he had purchased for various hobby interests. After a number of years he had to move the overflow into an old barn on the back of his lot. On the pretense that he might want to return to one of the hobbies he would never dispose of any of the equipment. He literally impoverished his family by these expensive experiments in various interests, which included among other things a large rock collection, a great deal of wood-working equipment, some expensive fishing tackle, a dark room full of photographic equipment, a lapidary wheel and an expensive loom for weaving rugs.

He suffered from a number of psychosomatic illnesses, which led him from one doctor to another until every physician in town hated to see him knock on the door. Periodically, this man would seek counseling from his clergyman, but would quickly lose interest in this also. He would then return to a pattern of blaming his problems on anyone except himself.

Closely akin to those seeking the so-called geographical cure are the people who receive clinical treatment or psychotherapy before they have hit what recovered alcoholics call the "bottom." Perhaps through the urging of friends or relatives or because they see some major part of their lives threatened by emotional immaturities, they are persuaded to seek help. They have not reached the point of being willing to correct their emotional patterns for the sake of their own inner integrity. A man who seeks help for his emotional problems *merely* to save his family or his job will not get well. The will to improve and to grow must come from the desire to make radical changes for the sake of one's own better self.

It is true that the man who is sick may be motivated to seek therapy in part by a desire to save his family. He may feel that for the sake of his children, he must do something about himself. But the real motivation must be based upon an earnest desire to become a better person. For the emotionally disturbed individual, things may frequently have progressed so far that the family life or the professional status is already destroyed. At the very least, these things may be greatly threatened. Nevertheless, each man must grow *within himself for himself*, not for any external gain which he hopes will come from his development.

Before a man can reconstruct his emotional life on any firm basis he must go to the very core of his own being, where he will fully appreciate his own aloneness. The process of emotional growth is such a rigorous discipline that, for a time, one must turn almost all of his thoughts inward. An almost complete focus of attention is required to affect any radical or permanent change.

In most things which we attempt, we can see some definite goal in sight. This goal assists us in our efforts. It also gives us some clues as to the methods we must use in achieving the goal. But the individual who is seeking emotional maturity does not know his goal. If he knew what it *felt like* to be in possession of a degree of emotional maturity he would not need to make the change. The person who starts out deliberately to seek the roots of his own self is reaching in the dark toward a development that he neither knows nor understands. He is going beyond his present to a totally unknown future. He is not even sure that the effort will be worthwhile. He knows with certainty that the present is unsatisfactory. He has somehow been led to believe that the future can be more satisfactory. He may have a vague idea of where he is going, but little notion of how he is to get there. Like Abraham in the Land of Ur, he sells his possessions of the past, liquidates all of his assets and goes out not knowing his destination.

No one likes to find himself in this kind of situation. No one will willingly seek it, unless he has reached the point of realizing that the past has been so completely unsatisfactory that he must take a chance of finding a better future. This is what is meant by "hitting bottom." The individual has reached the end of all his own resources. He has decided that he would rather die than remain as he is. He is willing to make *any* change which is necessary to achieve his end. Possessions, position, in fact everything which he has, must be regarded as secondary. Health and peace of mind are what he seeks. Inner serenity is his goal, but he can have many hours of doubt as to whether any of these things will be achieved.

It is as though a man were stripped naked of all the past and of all that he has achieved. In order to attain his vaguely comprehended objective, he is willing to bare his soul down to the inner core in a process of self examination. The person who makes this kind of a start has a very good chance of achieving all the things which he desires. On the other hand, if he cannot bring himself to seek emotional growth above all else, his chances of achieving it are very poor.

False pride plays a very large part in all of the obstacles to emotional growth we have mentioned. False pride clings to a part of the old self. False pride seeks to maintain a part of the old self unchanged. It is the thing which makes us say, "I want peace of mind, *but*—." There can be no "ifs" and no qualifications for the individual striving for maturity. Successful living demands many compromises, but a man cannot compromise with himself if he is to find his inner serenity.

This is a choice that only one person can make—the

person who is involved. No one can make it for him. No one will push him into it. It is his decision to make. If he does not make it, the universe will batter him against the hard wall of his own frustrations. He will be beaten senseless by emotional pressures of his own creating. His problems will continue with him unabated, while the years roll along bringing less and less vitality with which to cope with realities. The universe leaves him no choice at this point. He can hit bottom and grow, or he can hang onto his little pretenses and decay.

Chapter XI

The Parable of the Empty Mind

We are often startled to discover the deep psychological insights contained in the teachings of Jesus. We are inclined to indulge ourselves in the conceit that wisdom originated with the discovery of scientific thought and that the psychological knowledge of man dated from the time of Freud.

One of Jesus' short stories describes what happens to a man or woman who makes a half-way start toward mental health. The story is phrased in the superstitious language commonly understood two thousand years ago, nevertheless its lesson is clear enough to any modern reader. For lack of a better name, I have chosen to call this story, "The Parable of the Empty Mind."

As recorded in the Gospel according to St. Matthew, it reads as follows:

> When the unclean spirit has gone out of a man, he passes through waterless places seeking rest, but he finds none. Then he says, 'I will return to my house from which I came.' And when he comes he finds it empty, swept and put in order, then he goes and brings with him seven other spirits more evil than himself, and they enter and dwell there; and the last state of that man becomes worse than the first.

In Jesus' time mental illness or emotional disturbance was thought to be the result of evil spirits which took possession of one's body. Jesus and his disciples were apparently able to give help to many people with these problems. They undoubtedly also observed that some individuals showed temporary improvement, only to fall back into a worse condition after a short time. The Parable of the Empty Mind is an attempt to describe those who make a beginning of a new way of life, only to return to their old ways of thinking.

We have a better understanding today of the causes underlying mental turmoil. We know that demon-possession is only the product of human imagination. We also know that human beings can create a weird variety of confusions without any aid from an imaginary supernatural world.

Nevertheless, after we have discounted the superstitious elements in this story, we find an important truth in its words. The truth is this: it is not enough for a person to have the undesirable patterns removed from his mind. He must also replace these things with constructive thoughts and actions. If he fails to occupy his newly-released energy with new and better thoughts, the mind will turn again to the old patterns with a stronger attachment than before. If he relapses to his former undesirable behavior, he will not slip into it gradually over a period of years. He will drop all the way back with a sharp, sickening jolt.

We are urgently faced with this problem, whether the rehabilitation of the troubled mind is effected through some sort of religious conversion, or with the aid of psychiatry, or by a combination of both.

Those whose emotional lives need renovating will go through some process by which their minds are freed from the conflicts which disturbed them in the past. They will find some way to obtain freedom from guilt feelings, resentments, fears and jealousy. Long-standing inner conflicts will be removed; the personality will become less egocentric.

Once these things are accomplished, a tremendous amount of mental energy will be released from two sources: first, that part of the mind which has been wrestling to maintain an uneasy equilibrium between various emotional conflicts will now be unoccupied; second, many old associations, interests and time-consuming activities, which formerly took thought and attention, will be discarded.

The result is mental capacity released from any immediate use.

Since the nature of an empty mind is to fill itself, new creative thoughts must quickly replace the discarded, undesirable patterns. To fail at this point is to slip backwards. The human mind will keep busy with something. Its tendency in this direction is so strong that we must give the mind something to do. If we fail to keep our mental capacity occupied with desirable thoughts, the mind will find activities of its own, even if those activities lead toward its own destruction. This is not because the mind is essentially bad, but only because the mind is a perpetual motion machine designed for continuous activity. If one fails to steer it, the mind will not stop running; it will only continue to operate—aimlessly, out of control and eventually destructively.

The mind freed of conflicts, fears, tensions and other negative emotions can be engaged immediately in such activities as the following:

1. A rapid and extensive growth in self-understanding

2. Development of new habits of emotional behavior which will satisfy basic needs better than the old, undesirable patterns

The Salvation Army in its skid-row city missions has learned this lesson well. The old formula in these missions was the application of soup, soap and salvation. But the workers found a high percentage of their rehabilitative efforts were lost. Like the man in Jesus' parable, their converts would go through a promising conversion experience, then in a few weeks they were back on dope, alcohol and destitution.

Today a different procedure is followed. The Salvation Army still seeks to achieve a monumental conversion experience in the man from skid-row. It takes a cataclysmic emotional upheaval to relieve a human wreck of his accumulated negative emotions. After the religious conversion, however, a trained psychiatric social worker is assigned to the case. The case is followed up for weeks or months, if need be. The convert is gradually led along the torturous path of his rehabilitation. He is taught to work again. He is perhaps introduced to Alcoholics Anonymous. He may be hospitalized to build up a body ravaged by abuse and neglect. He is encouraged to use his released mental energy in constructive ways that will lead him toward independence, respectability and new acquaintances.

First, they get the skid-row out of the man, then they get the man out of the skid-row.

The result of this program is a much higher recovery rate and a great reduction in the number who suffer relapse.

A person who has spent years getting his mental processes confused will not straighten out the mess by experiencing one momentary flash of self-honesty. Permanent restoration will require continued effort, plus the patient understanding help of those who can tolerate his occasional slips without losing patience with the long-range process.

The mind of the troubled person is not an empty mind. It is full of thoughts, but they are disorganized and often in conflict with each other. The person who suffers from insomnia at night does not have a vacant head. He is troubled by too many thoughts, which keep him in a state of wakefulness. Because his thoughts were confused and hurried during the day, they continue in a torrent when he lies down for sleep at night.

We do not solve our mental problems by halting the activity of the mind. Temporary relief can be secured by drugs and alcohol, after which our minds resume their hurried wanderings when the effect of the sedation is exhausted. Neither is it enough merely to empty our heads of erroneous thinking. The constructive way is to replace destructive thoughts with ways of thinking that are in line with our new self-honesty.

How one accomplishes such a task is for each man to discover for himself. No one can diagram for another individual the way to achieve a positive mental pattern. If we were able to outline a standard procedure which would work for everyone else, then *everyone* with ordinary mental and emotional problems would get well if he wished.

However, there are a few guideposts we can erect for those who seek to fill their minds with more desirable thoughts.

First, one should set aside some time for thought and relaxation. A great many people stumble at this first hurdle. They want to improve, but they "do not have the time." They seek a happier way of life, but they are unwilling to make the effort. They would rather have a bit of advice in a capsule form, which can be mentally swallowed and forgotten. Or perhaps they imagine that just wishing for an untroubled mind is sufficient exercise.

A few years ago I had forgotten how to relax. I seldom had a night of uninterrupted, untroubled sleep. If I did sleep soundly, it was to awake nearly as tired as the night before. Tension remained unconsciously in my muscles during the sleeping hours. It became necessary that I relearn the art of relaxation with which nature endows the small child.

Like most people, I had read several books giving suggestions for relaxing the body, BUT I HAD NEVER PRACTICED ANY OF THE EXERCISES. I thought that simply reading the books should be sufficient for any intelligent person. My mind grasped the theory, but I still could not relax.

What I failed to realize was this: for years I had been teaching my body to be tense. I could not now teach my muscles to release their tension by telling them to relax. When it became apparent that I would either have to relax or resign myself to being ill most of the time, I took the first necessary step. I set aside two half-hour periods each day to practice muscle relaxation. I used the method outlined so well by David Harold Fink in his book, "Release From Nervous Tension." After following this schedule closely for twenty weeks I had again learned how to relax and could sleep restfully at night. The program yielded an unexpected dividend. I can now feel well with an average of two hours less sleep each night.

The time set aside to practice relaxation has been returned many times over in extra waking hours!

Just as training of the body takes time, so re-training the mind cannot be accomplished without giving some time to the matter. Every normal person can profit by setting time aside for quiet thought each day. For one whose whole pattern of thought must be changed, it is even more essential to find time to be alone and undisturbed.

A paper and a pencil are most useful during such times of solitude. One can destroy the scribblings after he has written them. But writing down one's thoughts about himself helps to keep the mind from evading the necessity for self-honesty. On some occasions, one may need to take an honest inventory of his motives and actions. At other times he may be tracing some emotional reaction to the lair of its childhood origins.

There are few techniques more useful than writing one's inner thoughts. It is a method closely related to the "free association" used by some psychanalysts. The mind is free to express itself without restraint—one thought leading quickly to another until the deeper motives are uncovered. Feelings and attitudes should be the main subject of such writing. To secure maximum value from the procedure one should record on paper the total picture of his feelings, however unflattering it may appear. Some people arrange a time each day which they set aside for these candid self-appraisals. The technique may also be profitably used in connection with counseling, especially when the hours made available by the therapist are limited. Thoughts put on paper have a way of becoming more clear. The mind is saved from aimless rambling and emotional pressure is discharged by this sort of expression.

These sessions alone with one's self will seldom flatter the ego. But they will develop the fearless ability to look one's self in the eye. They will help avoid mental confusion and the storms which threaten one's peace of mind.

A second suggestion is to make a habit of reading

something inspirational during the day. Some people like the Bible for this sort of reading. Others prefer a bit of poetry. Whatever the choice, everyone should expose himself at least once a day to a thought, a picture or some music which will lift him out of himself and help restore his perspective. A dull mind is almost as fatal as a cluttered mind. Dullness of mind can be produced by simply drudging along with ordinary thoughts all day and all month.

Third, learn to use your best mental powers upon the thoughts most interesting and helpful *TO YOU*. A mind often gets cluttered because we collect thoughts like a packrat collects junk. Or, we fill our mental storage place with interesting, but useless, items like an old man storing odd bits of household items in an attic.

We have all seen those filler items in small town newspapers, such as "the Leaning Tower of Pisa today is 16 feet out of plumb." Get enough such items in a newspaper and it becomes so cluttered the editor loses track of the news. The same thing happens when a human head collects too many unorganized interests. Clutter the mind sufficiently and you will lose your sense of direction, along with your ability to think.

Keep your mind busy upon the things most important to you. Resist the friends who feel you should be interested in some new thing just because they have found it interesting.

The human mind is man's best tool. He has not yet explored all its possibilities. But an improved mind is within the grasp of anyone. There is no exercise so rewarding as the excitement of exploring the potentialities of one's own mind.

Chapter XII

Constructive Anger

Anger is an explosive emotion. It is the atomic reaction of the mind. We are taught that the emotion should be suppressed or controlled. We have learned to think of rage as an undesirable emotion. It often causes us to do or to say things which we later regret. It places us in a position of disadvantage in the presence of those who keep their tempers.

Our efforts at controlling anger are usually not very effective. No emotion causes us more embarrassment, and most of the advice that is given about anger is ineffective. It is ineffective advice because it is impractical.

Unlike the genie in the bottle, explosive emotions cannot be controlled by putting them inside a sealed container. Sooner or later the cork will blow out of the bottle and a monster of hate and rebellion will emerge.

One of the better ways to handle undesirable emotions is to learn ways of diverting them into new and useful channels. For instance, the energy of irritations can be channeled into compassionate understanding.

Anger can be used constructively. The primitive savage had good use for his anger. His environment made it necessary for him to run or fight in cases of emergency. If he became angry, he soon worked off the emotion in the struggle for survival. Without it, he would not have been able to survive in the world of uncontrolled natural forces. He fought with his fellows for the small amount of available food and shelter. He was forced to defend his household against the raids of other savages and the threat of extinction by wild beasts. There was no orderly society, no police force, no courts of law which could protect him against extinction. Often he was saved from disaster by the additional energy made available through the mechanism of anger. After the emergency had passed, he was exhausted and relaxed. Suppression or control of these inner forces was not necessary. They were discharged in the immediate struggles for survival.

Modern man, on the other hand, has very little outlet for his anger. A food supply is as close as the modern grocery store. There is protection against criminal assault by the laws of society. Mechanical conveniences have reduced the number of emergencies to be faced in daily living. Except in the emergency of war or similar crises, there is no normal outlet for the emotion of anger. In the modern environment there is little opportunity to vent the violence of sudden rage without suffering social disapproval. The individual who frequently becomes angry on the job is considered a menace to his organization. If his boss makes him angry, he dares not show his feelings. If he goes to a party and some man becomes insultingly attentive to his wife, he is considered crude if he makes a scene in public. The more civilized the society, the less opportunities there are for the immediate expression of the feelings which the savage considered normal. Yet these emotions are present within us.

Under these conditions, the suppression and control of anger and resentment became a necessary art of civilized people. Civilization has placed a veneer over the savage interior, but the feelings are still present. Once we become angry, the energy must be discharged somehow. It cannot and should not be ignored. Unexpressed, its explosive force will either burst the seams of outward composure, or find its outlet in a twisted personality.

Anger is not an emotion that can be turned on and off at will. Once we become angry, adrenalin is forced into the blood stream, the heart beat quickens, processes in the gastrointestinal tract slow down, the muscles become tense and a variety of physical changes take place within the body which must somehow be expressed.

Obviously, we cannot return to primative savagery. We must live in the world as we see it. We do not wish to be considered social misfits, neither can we afford suppressed emotions which, at their worst, can make us raging homicidal criminals.

It has been suggested by many people that anger can be replaced by the feeling of love. "Love thy neighbor," the Bible says. We have taken this to mean that if we can love people enough they will not anger us. This is true in a very profound sense. But like all great principles of living, most of us do not know how to apply it. In attempting to meet anger by loving our neighbors, we often only succeed in further denial of an emotion which still exists within us.

How, then, can we use this powerful emotion constructively? Is there any use to which it can be put?

Primitive man used anger to solve his problems. Modern man can harness anger to help solve his problems. The world is full of explosive forces. The explosive force in gasoline can blow up a building or it can be used to drive an automobile. Dynamite is a dangerous substance in the hands of a fool, but without it the great skyscrapers of our cities, the beautiful highways over which we travel and the mines from which we obtain our metals would be impossible. The newest discovery of explosive force is the atomic reaction. Properly used all these forces give us sources of great power which can be used to benefit mankind. Improperly used they can destroy us. Such forces are only disastrous when they are exploded at the wrong time or in the wrong place. An atomic reaction can blow up a city or, properly released, it can furnish light and power for that same city. Mankind has made vast progress in his knowledge of the proper uses of these tremendous explosive forces.

Likewise, we must discover new and better ways for

114

controlling the explosive forces of our anger, or these forces will destroy us. When we speak here of anger, we are not talking about the momentary flashes of irritation which we all feel. These can be controlled or laughed off. We are speaking of real and deep-felt rage at some person or situation. We are talking about the kind of anger which cannot be handled by simply counting to ten. Most attempts to control anger are simply efforts at toughening the case within which it is held. They are attempts to contain an emotion that is seething inside us. This is not control—it is containment. *Real control implies intelligent constructive use of a force.*

In learning to control anger it is necessary to slow the reaction of the explosion. The anger has been caused by some person or situation which threatens us. Since we are threatened, we have a problem to solve. Instead of striking out blindly at people in the heat of temper, we should say to ourselves at the first onset of emotion, "I will now try to use this energy to solve my problems." This is good common sense. Any problem or any person which makes us angry confronts us with a situation of difficulty. The difficulty is such that we cannot solve it with ordinary energy, otherwise we would have done something about it long ago. Why not use this extra surge of energy to find a solution? Instead of trying to fight for control of the anger, store it up and let it drain off gradually in an extraordinary concentration upon the problem. Harness the energy. Use it to meet the crisis. Make the anger serve our purpose instead of serving the purposes of the anger. This is not as difficult as it sounds.

A very good friend recently told me about the first major test he had faced in harnessing the power of his anger. He is a man whose emotional immaturities had led him into alcoholism, alternating with a high dependence upon drugs. For fifteen years he had been unable to hold a steady job, in spite of the fact that he was an intelligent, likeable and well-educated man. Finally, after his problems had ruined his health and nearly cost his life, he secured help from a psychiatrist in a clinic. He achieved a self-understanding which enabled him again to become a useful citizen, and he secured a modest job with a firm in his home town. After a short time he found himself promoted to assistant manager in this firm.

One day, about three years after his rehabilitation, a situation arose which taxed his newly-found maturity to the limit. The manager, under whom he worked, became angry at a number of incidents which occurred on the job. Not being able to face the blame for the situation, the manager turned to my friend in a rage and unjustly accused him of mismanagement. In former days my friend would have replied with the sharp sarcasm for which he was noted. On this occasion, however, he decided to face the situation by trying to *use* his anger. He kept his tongue, not simply through an effort to contain his feelings, but in order to conserve the emotion for the solution of the problem. Obviously, the problem was the relationship with his supervisor. Instead of striking back immediately, my friend refrained from making any comment. He then started using the energy of anger to do some furious thinking about the situation.

First, he analyzed his own feelings, tracing each emotion back to its basic source within himself. He recalled the days before his rehabilitation and re-examined the present reaction as it was related to old immaturities. Former fears and insecurities were reviewed to see which of these threats to peace of mind were distorting his present objectivity. With perspective restored by a period of self-examination he began to see his role more clearly.

After a day of such thought, he came to the realization that his boss had emotional problems of his own which had caused the reaction. With this understanding came a new insight about their relationship. By this time, he had managed to exhaust the energy of the anger in thinking constructively about the problem.

He made an appointment with the manager in private, and was able to discuss the incident in an atmosphere of calm good humor. The employer was beginning to feel extremely guilty for his part in the incident. My friend assured him that he felt no resentment. Within five minutes the supervisor was talking about *his* problems and my friend listened with a sincere interest for over an hour. By the end of the discussion, the supervisor was asking for help in learning to handle his own emotions in a better fashion.

Out of this incident came a deeper friendship and respect. The manager was helped to achieve a better understanding of himself, while my friend was jubilant over his first experiment in learning to use the emotion of anger.

A great aid in controlling anger in this fashion is the ability to inject humor into the situation. At times all of us face tremendous problems in our lives. When these problems produce anger, we can find in the emotion a force for extraordinary solutions to extraordinary problems. Thus, the anger is discharged, there is no room for the retention of resentment, and we will have discovered a whole new resource for successful living.

The same principles apply even when anger is not justified. Sometimes our anger is only an expression of thwarted immaturities. There is no outward reason why we should become enraged. In some cases, we can use the energy of rage for a period of concentrated thinking about ourselves. Then the constructive action will be used to obtain deeper self-understanding. Whether our problem is internal or external, we can use our rage as a source of power and stimulation for the high concentration of thought which is necessary to solve our difficulties. Most of the time we do not think very hard about anything. Yet, in our modern world, we are faced with situations which require concentration of a very high order. The savage used his anger for extraordinary physical exertion. The modern man can use his for extraordinary mental concentration. If we will learn to direct anger in this fashion, we can raise our mental powers to a furious pitch which will surprise us by its results. *Our mental powers and our emotional energies will combine* to produce results of which we had never dreamed ourselves capable.

We have called this chapter "Constructive Anger." It would have been just as appropriate to have named it "How to Get Angry and Enjoy It." Whenever we are able to discipline any of our native powers for better constructive living, we will find a new joy in accomplishment, a new strength in successful living. Like the long-distance runner who has learned to get his second wind, we will have discovered one more way in which we can harness the tremendous unused powers which lie within us all. The truly great leaders of the world's history were not only men of superior character. They were also men who had learned to live with a larger *capacity* than most of us. The indignation of Jesus is a case at point. He not only knew how to love constructively, He also knew *what* things to hate and *how* to harness that anger for constructive use.

The art of increasing the capacity of the mind for creative production is largely contained in learning to redirect the emotional forces possessed by all of us. It is a great accomplishment when a troubled mind achieves a comfortable sanity. But the process of growth need not stop here. Further self-discipline and self-understanding will release ever-increasing energies for creative living. The greatest fulfillment of emotional growth lies in its possibilities for the enlargement of human capacity. The resulting transformation of some personalities is often so great that the difference we observe in the "before" and "after" appearances of their lives is startling. To harness the power of the more explosive emotions is to open the gate to an enlarged life.

Chapter XIII

Breathe Through Your Mouth

Too often satisfactory living is measured upon the scales of material success. The house, the car, the well-paying position are taken to indicate a person at peace with himself and the world.

When an apparently successful man suddenly shocks us by committing suicide, the comment is often heard, "Why did he do it? He had everything to live for!"

Did he? Perhaps it seemed so. But he must have been terribly desperate and sick inside to have found taking his own life the only way out. What was the matter? Where was the flaw? Usually we do not know the answer. It is too late to find the answer.

Perhaps part of the solution may lie in that penetrating statement from Frank M. Colby, a portion of which we quoted in another chapter. The full sentence reads as follows:

> In public we say the race is to the strongest;
> in private we know that a lopsided man runs
> the fastest along the little sidehills of success.

This is not to say that every successful man is a little bit crazy. However, those who appear most adept in their pursuit of "success" are often individuals whose personality demands that they seek success above all else. Those who exaggerate the importance of success may be found striving for the pinnacles in any area of life. Their ladder of success may be built upon the making of money, the desire for power or the need for professional status.

They are driven men—propelled by their own inner needs to seek a goal which excludes all other interests. Family, sports, community interests, peace of mind and intellectual activities are only considered in the light of their contribution to the main goal—personal success.

Ambition is a commendable thing. It is only a detriment when it becomes the compensation for a lopsided personality. Success is good also but, when it is sought in and for itself, it has the power to hide our eyes from an honest appraisal of ourselves.

Success so pursued can indicate a sick, compulsive personality. The alcoholic is driven by a compulsion. His peculiarity bears the stigma of social disapproval. Therefore, we find it easy to recognize that he is a sick man. In a way he is fortunate. He finds it hard to get through life without having it forcibly called to his attention that he is a misfit. He may be forced to seek therapy because society is intolerant of his immaturity.

But our pity should also go to the man whose twisted personality results in a *compulsion* to make money. His illness is also in the mind, but the making and saving of money is socially approved. Therefore, it will pass as a virtue, rather than an indication of emotional sickness. Faced with dire economic loss, such a man's inner world can collapse. Without the balance wheel of his compulsion to make money he is thrown back upon his fragile inner resources.

We need to learn that strong compulsions in any form are indicators of immaturity. It does not matter whether these compulsions happen to be socially acceptable. The compulsion to succeed can create quite as much heartache to a family and forebode as complete a nervous breakdown as alcoholism. Our admiration for success often blinds us to these deeper considerations.

Once we are aware of these dangers, we can consider more realistically some of the constructive things to be said for success. No one in his complete right mind wishes failure. Serenity and peace of mind should produce a condition which makes success at one's work a natural thing. Success, in and for itself, will not be the principal goal. At the same time, the habit of success should come as easily as breathing.

There is a very great and profound statement to this effect in the teachings of Jesus. He had been describing the folly of giving one's primary loyalty to material things. In conclusion he said, "But seek first the kingdom of God and his righteousness, and all these other things shall be added unto you."

Live right, think right, get rid of your egocentricity, and good things will happen to you.

It is a thrilling experience to sit in an Alcoholics Anonymous meeting and listen to the life stories of those who have been sober for a few years. They will tell of the years of debt, of losing one job after another, of broken homes and a succession of various troubles. Then, finally, comes the day when sobriety is achieved. They came to the point where sobriety and correct thinking became the most important goal in life. As their stories unfold a look of almost childlike unbelief comes to their faces as they say something like this, "—and now I have a home, a good job and a car that is all paid for."

There is a success which comes as a by-product of emotional growth and the habit of serenity.

My own awareness of this kind of success began on the day when a psychiatrist told me, "Learn to breathe through your mouth."

I had always been one of those individuals who does everything the hard way. I had enjoyed a reasonable amount of success but only with prodigious effort, and always with the feeling that life was an uphill struggle. That one could succeed by relaxing was an entirely foreign idea to my thinking. The notion that the way to get things done was through struggle for every worthwhile goal had been deeply ingrained. It had never occurred to me that there was any other way to accomplish the desired goals in life. Still, upon occasion, I realized I was spending a great amount of effort to produce such limited results. Since that day in the psychiatrist's office I have been trying to "breathe through my mouth." At times the results have been startling.

We have known a few people whose every action seems attended by good fortune. Whatever they do appears to be blessed with success. On the other hand, some of our acquaintances are continually encountering failure. First one thing and then another goes wrong. Even when their efforts seem to be intelligently planned, unfortunate circumstances bring disaster.

We have dismissed these puzzling circumstances by calling the first group lucky and the second unlucky. Unquestionably, chance does play a large part in all our lives. Nevertheless, why is it that some people are nearly always able to turn chance to their advantage, while others encounter one defeat after another in spite of fortuitous circumstances?

A clue has been found in the psychological discovery that some people are accident prone. We have found that the emotional climate of one's mind has a profound effect upon one's ability to avoid accident. Conversely, we have found that some people are successful in most things they do because they have learned to maintain an inner mental climate which has been sometimes called "thinking success."

How does one learn to think success? What are the essential mental elements possessed by some people which enable them to meet both the crises of life and the daily grind of routine with more success than others?

Perhaps the first thing which characterizes the truly successful person is a strange kind of indifference to success, as such. Unfortunately, success in our American culture has too often been defined in terms of gadgets. A man is called a success when he can afford an expensive automobile, a plush residence in the suburbs, a house full of electrical appliances and an impressive desk in an office decorated in expensive fabrics and plastic. Such things are not the measure of the kind of success about which we are speaking. The American success ladder is a good thing in the sense that men should be free to fall and rise vertically within a free society. It is a bad thing when the securing of success in terms of things becomes a substitute for inner self-knowledge and for the inner satisfaction of being a worthwhile person in one's own small niche.

Success, defined in the way we wish to find it, is that quality of mind which enables a man to confront a problem with ease and arrive at a relaxed solution most satisfactory to himself and most serviceable to the rest of mankind. Success should not be sought primarily for itself, anymore than happiness should be sought as a goal apart from true serenity. Those who are successful in this sense are people who are doing that which they most enjoy doing. They are individuals who are doing what functionally fits them. They have taken an inventory of their talents and abilities and within the framework of this inventory they have built occupations which closely fit their own personalities. First of all they are successful people within their own minds—successful in the sense that their true selves are expressed in their work, in their home life and in their friendships. They are individuals who have learned to know themselves well enough to know their limitations as well as their strengths. Whatever their talents may be, they have concentrated upon these abilities. They do not waste their time doing things outside the main stream. The things that they choose *not to do* may not be trivial, they are simply things which will divert energy and attention from the main stream. Above all, they are people who seek to serve humanity in the best way that they can. They do not waste energy in vain envy of those whose service lies in other fields.

A second thing which characterizes the truly successful individuals is the ability to serve humanity without attempting to build the ego in being of service. They care very little about what people think, considering it to be of far greater importance whether their work is pleasing in their own eyes. They wish to do all things well, but they are their own most severe critics.

To be successful in living, one must not tie his hopes too tightly to any particular objective. He must not feel that failure in one area means total failure. Outward triumph or defeat must not conquer the inner purpose around which life is built. When one feels that a set course of action is right for him, he must not let temporary failure distract him from it. *Neither can he permit the security of quick success to divert him from the course which seems at the moment unproductive.* After one has taken inventory of his resources, there will come times when risks must be assumed, when all the gains must be assembled into one stake and everything gambled upon the conviction that the course is right.

We often see people who make an apparent success by slamming through life like a bull through the china shop. They care not upon whose toes they may tread. Everything is sacrificed to the desire to get ahead. These are the compulsive personalities. Early childhood training often seems directed toward the production of this kind of person. There is a little doggerel verse by an unknown author which well expresses this kind of training. It is called, "The Modern Man."

> Hurry the baby as fast as you can,
> Hurry him, worry him, make him a man.
> Off with his baby clothes, get him in pants,
> Feed him on brain foods and make him advance.
> Hustle him, soon as he's able to walk,
> Into grammar school; cram him with talk,
> Fill his poor head full of figures and facts,
> Keep on a-jamming them in till it cracks.
> Once boys grew up at a rational rate,
> Now we develop a man while you wait.
> Rush him through college; compel him to grab
> Of every known subject, a dip and a dab.
> Get him in business, and after the cash,
> All by the time he can grow a mustache;
> Let him forget he was ever a boy,
> Make gold his god and its jingle his joy.
> Keep him a-hustling and clear out of breath,
> Until he wins—nervous prostration and death.

124

We do not need to go far outside our circle of immediate friends to find individuals whose lives and whose health have been wrecked upon the rocks of such success dreams. Happy the man who has been forced at an early age to face the futility of this kind of hectic living. He will be a *person* after such an experience. He will know it is more important to *be* someone than it is to *do* something. He will be forced to discover within himself the tools by which he can create the kind of relaxed tension by which true success is achieved.

One who has the habit of success is like a man who walks down a corridor or hallway, along which there are doors on both sides. He does not always know which door he should enter, but as he goes down that hallway, gently pushing at each door, he will eventually find one which will swing open easily. If it swings open, he can take a peek inside and see if it is the room he wishes to enter. But if he comes to a door which does not respond to a gentle push, he does not stand there and batter futilely at it with his fists. If it does not open easily, he knows it is either not *the door* that he should enter or it is not the *time* to go through it.

To take this attitude toward life, one must have a belief in the goodness of the universe. He must have a faith that there are certain courses of action at certain times which are profitable. There are other courses of action which can only lead to disaster. The man who believes that he designs his own future in his own limited wisdom will never be content to live in this fashion. It requires a person who has faith in the universe, as well as faith in himself. There must be the conviction that the purposes of one's life are best served when he is going along the lines of the main stream of the universe. He must know that if he thinks right and stays relaxed, trying to do his best each day, that the universe will provide the best he is capable of receiving.

Such a philosophy will not obliterate the limitations of life, for acceptance of these boundaries is part of the peace of mind which goes with successful living. There are limitations which are placed upon our strength. We are not all able to do the same amount of work. Age and physical condition play a large part in the amount of effort we have to give.

Time is another boundary. Few of us live productive lives beyond the age of eighty. Within that brief span there is only a certain number of activities in which one can engage. A person who attempts to do *everything* in eighty years is a fool. He must choose those activities for which he has time.

There are the limitations of geography. Modern transportation has enabled us to cover great distances, but man has not yet been able to devise a method by which he can be in two places at once.

He is restricted also by hereditary equipment—mentally and physically. Mental capacity is largely fixed at birth. It is true that many people, who have been born relatively weak in certain physical ways, have done a great deal to strengthen their powers, but the body can progress only so far in spite of all exercise. The acceptance of such limitations is a necessary part of the mental conditioning for success.

Many people fail to make the maximum success of which they are capable because of the fear of possible failure. They want success so much that they cannot risk defeat. Psychological literature is full of case histories of individuals who have attempted to succeed in some profession only to be the cause of their own premature defeat.

A good example of this was the young man who studied law in preparation for a bar examination. He felt that failure in his profession would mean the disapproval of his father. Subconsciously he always arranged in some way to fail his bar examination. His failure at this point enabled him to escape the possibility of later failure in practice. After he had seen a psychiatrist and discovered that the fear of his father's disapproval prevented him from doing his best, he was able to pass examination with no difficulty and is now doing very well in his chosen work.

Some people fail because they attempt too much. Other people fail, as we have just suggested, because of the fear of some kind of disapproval. Still other people fail because they are square pegs in round holes, trying to do something for which they are not equipped.

Whatever formula for success we may devise must fit our own needs. When the going is hard, when the obstacles seem insurmountable, when we find ourselves panting through life after something which constantly eludes our grasp; that is the time to pause in the mad rush and breathe through our mouths.

Chapter XIV

Pain — The Partner of Growth

In his thoughtful book, "Pain, Sex and Time," Gerald Heard discusses the relationship between pain and the possibility of man's further growth. He suggests that in his capacity for pain man has inner resources which incline him toward an upward spiral of mental advancement.

It is not normal for a person to enjoy pain. People who go out of their way to invite life to give them a beating are seeking a kind of painful pleasure as a compensation for some dissatisfaction they feel within themselves. To them pain has become necessary. They are unable to feel complete unless they are being hurt or anticipating the possibility of being hurt. An example is the hypochondriac who surrounds himself with bottles of pills and lives in a state of chronic anticipation of becoming sick.

For most of us, however, pain is an unwelcome guest. We do not like to be hurt. We avoid suffering and discomfort whenever possible.

In spite of our efforts, we cannot escape our own nerve endings. Neither can we avoid all circumstances that will bring us mental and physical anguish. Occasionally, in spite of all our precautions, we will be hurt. When unavoidable pain does come, it will not contribute to our growth unless we learn to use it.

We all know some individuals who have become better people because they learned how to accept pain and use its agony in a positive, constructive manner. Several members of our community lost sons in World War II. There was one father who will always be remembered by those who knew him. He and his wife had two sons in the Armed Forces and a younger daughter at home. The members of this family were especially close to one another. They shared each other's activities to a marked degree. One of the boys was lost in the Pacific Theatre of operations. The shock must have been felt deeply by both parents, but all those close to the family felt that the loss was more deeply experienced by the father. In the death of his son he lost both a child and a very dear friend. It was that kind of a relationship between them.

When the news arrived we were all concerned for this lonely man. We need not have worried. The same kindness, strength and good sense which had made him an exceptional father enabled him to accept the pain and make the best possible use of it.

As the months went by this very wonderful man became an even more remarkable presonality. He continued to give his deep understanding and comradeship to the son and the daughter left to him. He lent support to his wife in her grief. His generous spirit and warm radiance were felt by every child, young person and adult who visited his home. He was tolerant of people almost past belief, yet there was no softness in his toleration. He made one feel at home in his house, yet one knew there was an inner privacy and dignity within the man, which no one dared invade.

There was only one explanation for his attitude. He had completely accepted the inevitable nature of the pain. At the same time he had used the experience to enable him to increase the quality of his day-by-day living. He got more from life than most of us because he put more of himself into it than some of us do.

We think of another friend who was suddenly crippled by rheumatoid arthritis. He is in constant and excruciating pain. Like many people with this disability, he lives partly on a diet of aspirin. He could have lain down and let the disease stiffen his joints. Instead, he has chosen to make use of the limitation brought by arthritis. He had always wanted to attend college, but never did so because of the need to support a family. Now that he can no longer work at the trade for which he is well trained, he has launched upon a four year course in preparation for a new life work. Thus, in his middle years he is using his disability to continue growth in a new direction.

Illustrations of people who have made pain an instrument of growth are not hard to find. More difficult to discover are the clues to why extreme pain overwhelms some individuals, while others use it to climb the stairs of personal development. There is no simple, single answer to this question. How one deals with the tendency to self-pity is part of the answer. That indefinable quality we call the will to live is another. Previous training, the philosophy of life, the kind of support given by family and friends are other factors affecting the outcome of disaster.

Pain tests the inner fortitude with results that are often surprising. No man can predict with certainty how much he can bear until he has borne it. Most of us have inner strength beyond our expectations. Again, there may be times when we are overcome by some pressure which we had previously scorned as trivial.

The finest source of strength in meeting pain and disaster is the sure knowledge that trouble *can be used*.

Quite often friends ask me about my experience with polio. They sincerely want to know how one reacts to physical disability. Walking with the aid of canes and a brace is very much like wearing false teeth. The one is no different than the other, except as to degree. False teeth may be troublesome at times, but they are not disabling. Dentures are far better than having no teeth at all.

As to the emotional pain of finding oneself suddenly and irrevocably deprived of normal muscles, I have only one answer for my inquiring friends. Through the years I have tried to use polio as a means of growth. If someone were to have the power to say, "I will give you back the strong, firm legs you had at twenty-eight in exchange for all the good things you have gained from having polio," I could only reply, "I cannot afford to trade on that basis."

About two years after polio struck I sat down one day to list all the advantages which had come to me from attempting to use the disability. The list filled two pages. Today, seventeen years after contracting the disease, the list would be enormous. I could not *afford* to trade all those gains in growth for merely regaining a pair of normal legs.

This fact does not make me feel brave or exceptional or virtuous. But I *know* beyond any inner doubt that pain can be used for growth. If suffering does come, as it will to everyone in time, we can do far more than simply endure it. Pain cannot be laughed off. It will not go away if we adopt an attitude of "eat, drink and be merry." Pain will be there, no matter how we seek to ignore or deny it. But pain which is accepted and used will compensate us with growth.

One does not need to be exceptionally strong or brave in order to use suffering. In fact, it may require more strength merely to endure pain than is needed to glean constructive gains from its presence. Those who have known real pain have also experienced deep fear and uncertainty. It is not strength or courage which will see us through a time of trouble, but rather such qualities as faith and hope and joy in living. We need always to think positively about our problems. We can never adopt a permanent attitude of feeling sorry for ourselves.

Some pain comes to us because of our own foolishness. Other pain results inevitably from being alive. As long as we live, death is with us. Hurting is an essential part of being alive. No infant ever learned to walk without taking some bumps. No young lover ever courted without some heartache. No student can master a subject without knowing the threat of failure. It is true that "man is born to trouble as the sparks fly upward." It is also true that man will grow as long as he has the will to use *all* his experiences—both the good and the bad.

However pain may come to us, whether by the course of events or through the effects of our own stupidity, it should be used as a means of teachings us the things we might not otherwise learn.

What are some of the ways we can use suffering?

First, suffering can be used to bring us closer to our fellow man. We can discover how much we share with all those who have known trouble. There is no closer bond between men than the knowledge of common sufferings and hurts. A doctor is a better physician to his patients after he has experienced illness and pain himself. A rehabilitation counselor is more effective in working with the physically handicapped if he has some disability over which he has gained a mastery.

During World War II a service organization employed a man born without arms to visit the amputee wards of veterans' hospitals. This remarkable person had learned to do most of the things a normal person would do. Instead of ordinary hose he wore a mitten-type sock on his feet. He would sit down in a cafe, slide the loafer shoe off one foot, bend one flexible leg around in front of him and pick up a fork or spoon between his toes. He would then proceed to eat his meal in such a natural manner that diners seated a few tables away would notice nothing unusual going on. It was especially startling to see him stand on one leg in a dormitory wash room and shave himself, holding the razor between his toes. He went from hospital to hospital demonstrating to amputees that life did not necessarily end with the loss of a limb. His example and understanding meant more to the patients than a thousand lectures by normal physiotherapists.

Whether we work with troubled people in a professional capacity or whether we know them as layman and friends, the suffering we have known will make us better people. Unless we have known pain and used pain to the best advantage, it will be difficult for us to become an understanding part of mankind's deeper feelings.

Pain which is experienced, but not used constructively, can make us bitter against life. To have known hurt is not enough to produce understanding of the hurts of others. Our reaction to pain, not the fact of pain itself, is the thing which determines whether our minds become more sweet or more sour.

Properly faced, pain can bring a deeper inner humility in our common humanity. It can make us more tolerant, less quick to judge others, more patient with the imperfections and failures of our acquaintances. It can bring us a more mellow personality than we knew before, or it can twist us toward a brittle, harsh kind of thinking.

The kindness of true understanding is not a smothering, false pity directed at the sufferer. Those who have often known extended periods of illness shudder when they remember the well-intentioned visitors who stood beside the bed with a "you-poor-thing" attitude. This is not kindness. Neither is it understanding. It is a form of egocentric superiority. It represents a need on the part of the visitor to feel superior because he is well, while the object of his pity is unfortunate enough to be lying ill.

True kindness goes far deeper—so deep that the sufferer immediately recognizes its sincerity. True kindness may sometimes prompt us to say firmly to the sufferer, "Quit feeling so sorry for yourself."

A second way in which we can use pain is to gain a better inventory of ourselves. Suffering batters us against some of the harder realities of the universe. It forces us to ask ourselves what things are truly important in life. In re-assessing our direction and our basic purposes we are brought closer to self-honesty about ourselves and our world.

Anyone who has been close to death will recall the clarity of insight which the experience brought to him. Some of the things which seemed very important are then seen to be trivial or non-essential. Suffering can teach us to channel our strength into those courses that are truly important. We sometimes find it necessary to drop from our lives those time-consuming activities which contribute little of permanent value to our growth.

Third, pain can bring the ability to wait. Most of us are in too much of a hurry. We think that furious activity will enable us to experience more, to appreciate more. This is not always true. For instance, suppose a person is walking rapidly down a busy, city sidewalk. He is moving at the same general speed as the other pedestrians going the same way. He will meet only the people going in the opposite direction. If he is looking for some particular individual, he will have a much better opportunity to see that person if he steps to the side of the traffic and lets the people going both ways pass by him.

There are times when we need to hurry. There are other occasions when life will bring us the best results if we have the patience to wait and let the stream of the universe flow past us.

We do not always save time by hurrying. If we must sometimes wait in order to be at the right place when our destiny approaches, then we are using the best method for saving our own time.

Patience can be acquired through suffering. It is reported that once on a political campaign train a reporter asked Franklin D. Roosevelt how he could remain so relaxed in the midst of the hectic, speech-filled trip across the country. Everyone except the President had shown signs of the pressure.

President Roosevelt is said to have smiled as he replied, "You are looking at a man who spent a year just trying to wiggle his big toe." There are those who strongly opposed Mr. Roosevelt for his political views, but those who knew him as a polio at Warm Springs Foundation all recognized that he had built great inner resources from the way he used the experience of polio.

These are only a few of the ways in which pain can be used to produce growth. The pain is not separate from its particular cause. Each hurt, each disability or disaster brings its unique opportunities for development. Blindness opens one field of possible growth. The death of a loved one brings a different set of circumstances. The pain of remorse presents still another challenge. Whatever may be the cause of pain, it is one of our greatest avenues toward making something better of ourselves.

To the remarkable growth possible through such channels is added an unexpected by-product. Those who have formed the habit of *using* pain discover that they are usually hurt less often than those who face suffering with any other method. Good things not only happen to them more frequently, but their willingness to accept life as it comes brings them added serenity in the time of disaster. They are less apt to regard a minor problem as a major catastrophe.

Good fortune is not so much a product of circumstances as it is a result of the manner in which we confront the varying events of life. Most of the things, which we label as disaster can be made to serve a useful purpose. At the very least, we can salvage from disastrous circumstances some value which will add growth and meaning to our lives.

Chapter XV

Home Remedies and Family First Aid

When a person is ill, his family can usually contribute much toward speedy recovery. In the case of mental illness, however, the role of a family is critical. The family's attitude sometimes spells the difference between the achievement of serenity and complete disaster.

Many mental clinics now make it a necessary part of therapy to educate the family on the subject of aftercare. Before the patient returns to normal community living the psychiatric social worker and the vocational counselor will work closely with his immediate family. It has been found that acquainting relatives with the emotional problem is one of the best ways of avoiding repeated returns for clinical or hospital care.

When family understanding is lacking, the difficulties for the emotionally disturbed person are vastly increased. The family has often become a part of the individual's problem. Popular articles on psychology have made us aware that most of our emotional problems are rooted in early childhood experiences. Present home situations of *adults* are often equally as damaging to mental health as any childhood difficulty.

People with emotional problems are apt to marry individuals whose emotional patterns irritate the "infection" of their own mental complexes. They marry each other for better or for worse, only to discover that marriage brings out the worst in both of them. As time adds to the original problems, which both partners brought to the marriage, communication becomes more difficult between them. Each knows all of the worst features of the other, for they are at their worst when they are alone together. They batter at one another's protective defenses until each becomes a stranger to the other's true thoughts and feelings.

Perhaps one member of the family finally has a nervous breakdown and goes to a hospital. This gives the remaining member of the marriage an opportunity to feel that he is the "normal" one. It may take considerable time and effort for a therapist to lead the "well" member of the family toward an understanding that he, too, is part of the problem. The whole family may have become so emotionally "infected" that each member may need a minor kind of therapy. They may not necessarily be the cause of the difficulty, but the years have brought many complex relationships which in many ways are detrimental to the calm companionship which we usually associate with a comfortable home. If families can recognize their own share in these complex relationships, they will then find it much easier to make the necessary adjustments which will, in the long run, bring increasing happiness to all members of the family group.

When a person secures professional help for some mental or emotional problem, there are usually experienced people available besides the psychiatric social worker to help the family understand the problem. Many psychiatrists themselves make it a practice to spend a great deal of time with the family of the patient. Family counselors, by the nature of their work, are deeply concerned. If the individual is an alcoholic, the family of some recovered alcoholic is usually available to assist the spouse and children toward better understanding in the essential nature of alcoholism.

However, this sort of help is not given in every case. The case load in clinics and the demands upon the time of those who are qualified to assist the emotionally disturbed are very heavy. Our society is producing emotional problems among us much more rapidly than we are training people for the necessary therapy. Consequently, a great many people who need help are unable to secure it. Even when therapy is available, families are sometimes given only a sketchy review of the problem. The ways in which they can assist toward ultimate and complete recovery are not always made clear to members of families.

Therefore, we shall try to offer some suggestions even though individual situations differ so greatly that we can only speak in the most general terms.

The one thing most needed, which the family can give, is acceptance. The person freshly returned from mental therapy, whether in a clinic or a hospital, is proud of his newly-found understanding and hopeful for the future. He is also frightened about the prospect of facing the members of his family and acquaintances in the community. The old emotional hurts have been cleansed and healed, but the scars are still red and swollen. He is extremely sensitive about his illness. The feeling of past shame and failure, the uncertainty about how he will be accepted, the fear of what people may say behind his back, are close to the surface of his mind.

At the clinic or the hospital he has met people with problems similar to his own. He felt at home among them. He was accepted. The professional staff has treated him with understanding. If the treatment was successful, he may be happy to escape from its rigorous discipline, but he has found within the hospital the kind of acceptance among fellow patients and doctors which he may not receive when he first returns to the more informal atmosphere of the community. He is not at all sure about his employer or the attitude of his family. He may have good reason to suspect that they will show little appreciation for his newly-found approach to living.

If he has been confined to a hospital as an in-patient, he will have a difficult time for a few days just prior to his release. He will probably go through a period of what patients sometimes call "pre-discharge jitters." Some of his older symptoms will return in a minor form. He has been wanting to go home but, now that he finds the prospect is imminent, he is afraid to leave the hospital.

At this critical period of discharge or release from treatment, families should show the utmost understanding. They must try to put behind them any personal hurts that may have resulted from pre-treatment experiences. They should do their best to welcome the patient into the home with love and acceptance.

In accepting a member of the family after therapy, a great deal of patience will be necessary. Temporary relapses may occur. One of my best friends in the fellowship of Alcoholics Anonymous tells of his wife's patience during a relapse to drinking that occurred several years ago. After an active period in Alcoholics Anonymous, he had taken a drink which led him quickly back to the old patterns of thinking and behavior. He would try to hide the smell of alcohol on his breath with chewing gum in the hope that his wife would not know he was drinking. This went on over a period of several months. She knew he was drinking, but said nothing about it. Never did he receive a word of re-crimination from his wife.

Finally, one day he reached the end of his own resources and he said to wife, "What would you think about my going back to Alcoholics Anonymous?"

His wife replied, "I think it would be a very good idea and I would be glad to go with you." She then came over to him and put her arms around his neck. For the first time since he had begun drinking she permitted herself to show emotion about his condition.

In telling this incident, my friend pointed out that he was the type of personality who, if his wife had shown any impatience, would only have stayed drunk that much longer. He would have felt the need to prove that he could manage his own life. This woman knew her husband very well. She recognized that *she* could not get him sober. He alone must make up his own mind that therapy was necessary. All that she could do was stand by patiently, giving him her love and acceptance, waiting until he was ready to make the necessary move toward sobriety.

Another problem, which makes it difficult for the family to show patience, is the commonly accepted notion that a person returning from an alcoholic clinic or mental treatment center is "cured." Emotional illnesses can be arrested—they cannot be cured. They are not infections which completely disappear with the destruction of some microscopic organism in the body. They are mal-functions of the mind. *There is nothing to prevent the mind from returning to its old pattern at any time when the individual fails to follow the wholesome thinking which arrested the condition in the first place.*

In this connection I have so often remembered a personal incident which occurred in my own home shortly after I returned from hospitalization for just such a condition. One evening, about three weeks after my return, some unusual pressures of the day (precipitated by an unwise remark of a medical doctor, whose training should have taught him more understanding with the emotionally disturbed) produced a flare-up of several old symptoms. I tried for several hours to get the situation under control. My wife's patience, already worn thin by months of strain, became exhausted. Finally, with a deeply despairing note in her voice, she said, "I thought you would come home without any of those symptoms." The realization that she was close to hysteria shocked me out of preoccupation with myself. I explained to her that the new understanding, which comes with therapy, only represents part of the recovery process. After therapy there must follow a tedious discipline of translating the new understanding into daily habit patterns. Thus assured, she was able to tolerate my minor upsets without becoming alarmed that they might foreshadow a major crisis.

Families who have long endured the peculiarities of their sick loved one, hope that mental therapy will produce a quick cure for these intolerable pressures. Common sense may tell them that miracles cannot be expected, but it takes more than intelligent common sense to keep them from wishing for a miracle.

Patience is easy for him who has not long been under

trial. But the erosion of repeated disappointment, daily uncertainty and chronic emotional pressures can wear down the resistance. Even after the fresh hope of treatment has made the future seem brighter, there is still only a thin amount of resistance against the return of impatience.

Emotional growth takes time. No person, however willing or intelligent he may be, can hurry this growth beyond a certain speed. The patience which we ordinarily give to people in our daily contacts must be extended to even greater limits when we are dealing with an individual who is trying desperately to recover from emotional illness.

Acceptance and patience are qualities which we have mentioned first, even ahead of understanding. The family will not always be able to understand the roots of the problem. Even under the best of circumstances, there may be elements of behavior which seem puzzling to them. If, however, they can give a high quality of acceptance and maintain a patient attitude, these things will mean more than any amount of understanding. Nevertheless, understanding is extremely important. Members of the family should try to increase their grasp of the basic causes or mechanism affecting the one they love. They can do this in a number of ways.

Beyond the explanations given by professional therapists, selected reading about the problem and its causes is often helpful. There is a wide range of literature available to the lay person on almost all emotional illnesses. The therapist can usually suggest those books which will be beneficial for the family. If the problem is alcoholism, Alcoholics Anonymous family groups can suggest literature of this nature. Any good public library can supply books on other subjects. Members of the family do not need to become "experts" in the field of psychology. Too wide a selection of reading will only produce confusion.

They can supplement this knowledge by talking to recovered people who have had the same problem. Families of those who have made successful recovery can help toward an understanding of the pitfalls to recovery. They can explain a great many of the reasons for behavior which seems peculiar.

Understanding is a valuable tool in another way. Without understanding, the loving family often makes the mistake of treating the returning patient as though he needed to be handled with kid gloves. This can be very damaging. It sets him apart from the rest of the family and makes him feel that his relatives doubt what little sanity he has gained. Undoubtedly, he will need some help, but if the family has an understanding of the problem they will know where to draw the line between help and too much help. They must learn to avoid the things that irritate, without continually asking in an overly-anxious tone, "What did we do wrong?" The returning patient does not wish to be protected under a bell jar. Neither does he wish to be turned loose from all reassurance. Above all, he wants to be treated like an individual, to be trusted, to be loved without being fawned over. He wants to be accepted as an adult with some judgment; to be given room in which to stretch and grow. If he feels that the family is peering at him anxiously, expecting him any moment to stub his emotional toe and fall flat in the middle of his old complexes, he may try to avoid their questions. He desperately needs the understanding of his family, but he will avoid them if their actions give the impression that they know nothing of his problem.

In all of this the family must be willing to accept and follow the advice and suggestions of those who truly know the nature of the problem. If there are things which they do not understand, it is better to leave the patient alone than to rush in with an overly-solicitous attitude.

The family should give the therapy a chance to promote emotional growth. This takes time. Presumably the patient has learned what he needs to do. He now needs a permissive atmosphere in which to do it. He will grow as fast as he can. It does no good to crowd the progress.

If there is a return of a real emotional crisis, then something will have to be done about it. As we have already suggested in the illustration of our friend, the alcoholic, if the mental problem involves a resistance against admitting confused thinking, the family will only do harm by rushing in with a suggestion that further treatment is needed. However, some people with emotional problems do not have this type of resistance and it may be possible in such cases for the family to move rather hastily in encouraging that expert help be secured before the situation becomes too critical.

If the other qualities that we have mentioned—patience, understanding, acceptance—are present to a high degree, the problem of what to do in a crisis will usually be met quite satisfactorily. If these qualities are not present, there is not much point in advising the family what to do. They will almost certainly become a handicap to progress.

It would not be appropriate to conclude without saying a word about the things that the family needs to do to protect their own emotions against shock. Living with an emotionally disturbed individual, especially if that person is not making satisfactory progress, can be a demoralizing experience. The family needs to recognize one essential fact. *Whether a person makes emotional growth or not is primarily his own responsibility.* If he wishes to grow, there are things that the family can do to help. If he is not ready to *admit* that he needs to grow, or deep down inside he does not *wish* to grow, there is nothing the family can do to persuade him toward mental health. Each man must decide for himself whether he will take the way of life or the way of death. Often I have had disturbed families come to me in distress because some relative refused to take the first steps toward therapy. Perhaps they have been afraid that he might carry out some of his threats of suicide. The best possible help should be given to a person who makes threats of this kind. Competent professional advice should be sought. Nevertheless, it is often necessary for families to realize that any man who is thoroughly intent upon suicide will be able to carry out his intention, regardless of any attempt on the part of friends or relatives to prevent his action.

A sick person cannot be forced into health. Members of families cannot graft decisiveness onto the personality of an individual who is indecisive. Families will only increase their emotional agony by feeling that they alone are responsible for the recovery of a loved one. If they are conscientious families, they will not be able to escape from this feeling of responsibility, but they must understand that *ultimately* each man stands or falls in his own shadow. They can lend a helping hand when it is requested. They cannot provide sinews and bone or muscles to those who, within themselves, do not wish to stand in the sunlight of life.

Chapter XVI

The World of Beginning Again

The descent to the bottom of one's own resources is a bruising and painful experience. The ascent from these depths requires patience, perseverance and determination of the highest order. Sometimes the progress seems slow beyond endurance. The results will hardly seem worth the effort. At other times great gains will be made in a few days or weeks.

Emotional growth comes like the physical growth of children. As someone has said, "They grow *up* a while; and then *out* a while." There will be occasions when no visible growth is apparent. Then, suddenly, as though the inner self had been accumulating strength for the next leap, there will come a quick expansion of obvious progress.

Every successful practitioner of counseling has seen this happen over and over again in his clients. For several interviews the client will seem to repeat much the same material in each session. Little progress will be made on the surface. Then one day the conversation will suddenly dip to deeper levels of feeling, Some particularly troubling emotional problem will push its way to the surface. The counselor will place his hand upon a central key to the personality. As he turns that key a whole flood of new understanding will come to the client.

His face will light up. His whole attitude will change. Perhaps he will say, "Now I understand. Why did I not see that before?"

To those of us who have been privileged to witness this sudden miracle of personality growth, there is no more won-

.rful experience. When it happens we feel what amounts to a sense of awe. We have seen the creation of something close to the center of life take place before our eyes. We are awed and a little frightened because we have had a share in the splendor of creation.

To those who have not witnessed this rapid growth of personality, our description may seem overdrawn. Indeed, it is not. How can one adequately describe the miracle of any birth or growth? Is it not even more miraculous when there is a personality rebirth of one whose life had degenerated to the point of wreckage?

The world of beginning again has opened its doors to these individuals. They have taken the first step from despair to hope. They have found a stairway from frustration to faith in themselves. They have found a way to be delivered from dope, from drink, from depression, or from delusion.

It is true that some experience the miracle of emotional growth and yet slip back into the trap of their former twisted thinking. It is also true that not every seed which sprouts in the forest produces a full grown tree. The hazards of growth are always present. But some do live and some do grow. Because there is death, we ought not to refuse the opportunity to believe in life.

To refuse to believe in the world of beginning again is not realism. It is blindness. All about us are growing numbers of those who have found in that world a new way of life. As they live among us, quietly pursuing their newly-found serenity, we begin to take them for granted. In a way, this is as it should be. They do not wish to be regarded as a breed apart from other men and women. But neither should we forget the meaning of their success as we observe those whose lives are headed for the wrecking yard of human failure. Bad news always attracts more attention than good news. A forest fire is more sensational than a grove of tall trees growing beautifully together.

Let us think more often of the growing things.

Those who have found their way to growth should not be ashamed to admit their former disasters. If they must still compensate for their previous collapse by pretending it did not happen, then they have not fully recovered from their illnesses. Furthermore, they are depriving someone else in trouble of the assistance he needs. To be ashamed of one's scars is to indulge in a form of inner dishonesty. It is flight from reality. No one is fooled by such self-deception except the person who practices it.

To belong to the world of beginning again is to join a happy company. It should lead to a new usefulness in helping the massive horde of humanity which has not yet found the way to serenity. One of the by-products of serenity is a deep inner joy. It finds expression in sharing all good things with others. To be merely sane is good, but it is not enough for any man. Serenity is only one more small step beyond sanity. Yet how many people go through the processes of emotional growth without taking this final step! When one has had a taste of serenity he will never be satisfied to exist upon a mere diet of routine sanity. He will not be content to live only at the level where he barely avoids the edge of disaster.

He will want to preserve that state of mind where joy can be found. This joy is not mere gaiety. It does not exist primarily in an atmosphere where cares and difficulties are absent. The inner calmness where true joy is produced will be a thing that lifts one through the troublesome days. Serenity is the resource for tough times—for occasions when the going is hard and hope flickers only faintly through the dark.

Again and again one may partially lose his way. He will find himself wandering again through the unfriendly corridors of his negative emotions. When this happens, however, he can recall the time when his mind first entered the world of beginning again. He can retrace his steps in the light of that memory and find the place where he took the wrong turn. It is surprising sometimes how quickly the light will return, how fine it feels to experience the old inner assurance and the upsurge of joy which comes with it.

Sometimes these temporary digressions into one's darker world are accompanied by a state of mind where

147

other people appear to be completely out of step. One's ego becomes so inflated that the faults of others are exaggerated. One feels that he is essentially right, while others are mostly wrong.

Beginning again must always start inside the mind and the emotions. We are all affected favorably or adversely by our circumstances, but when we fail internally we lose much of our power to mold circumstances. Internal failure occurs long before its outward signs become apparent. Conversely, internal serenity is not always noticed immediately in any radical difference of behavior and manner. Time, however, always brings its rewards or its punishments. The man who lives to himself will eventually die by himself. The one who reaches out in sharing with others, will not cease to be a growing part of us all when he dies.

Those who enter into the serene way of life through the world of beginning again will find an ever-widening appreciation for all that is satisfying and enduring. Trees will seem more lovely. Grass will appear greener. Hills will inspire and the little roads which wind over them will give more pleasure as one travels. People will again become interesting.

A sunset is only beautiful to those who take the trouble to really see it. Appreciation of life is only possible to those whose emotional vision is unclouded by preoccupation with the problems of self.

To begin again does not mean a sudden return to all that is good. Neither does it mean that a whole life is transformed overnight. A man is not judged by whether or not he stumbles. A man can only judge himself by the *direction* he travels. To arrive is not important. To travel in the right direction, making a little progress every day, is the true test of life. Man's search is never done. Man's progress within the inner mind is never finished. Those who imagine they have arrived are the ones who have not really started. To think otherwise is to deny that part of life which commands us to continue growing without limit.

The business of growth is the only thing which can be pursued through a whole lifetime without inducing *a* feeling of boredom. Things lose their appeal. Ideas become commonplace. People come and go. But growth always remains exciting—full of surprises, full of promise. To remain in the world of beginning again one must continue to make the effort to grow. The alternative is slow death. We do not know why this is true. We cannot always give a satisfactory answer to the ultimate purpose behind human life. But those who have lost their way in the darkness of inner fear have found that the alternative to growth is indescribable hell. Avoiding a return to this abyss is reason enough for them to continue in their efforts. One may say that their reason is selfish, but it pays returns in a coin called serenity. They hope to be useful, but they do not often ask, "Am I useful?" They have found a technique of living which escapes hell and often brings a little touch of heaven. This is reward enough. This is reason enough for growing.

It is a way of life which also makes the world a little better place in which others can live. No man can rightfully aspire to more than this.

The search is yours and mine.
Each finds his way with help,
But yet alone.

Serenity is the goal.

It comes to those who learn to wait
And grow;
For each can learn to understand himself
And say, "I've found a
Joy in being I,
And knowing you;
A knowledge of the depths I can descend,
A chance to climb the heights above my head."

The way is not so easy all the time.
Our feet will stumble often as we go.
A friend may need to give some extra help,
As we once gave to others
When in the hour of fear.
This is no picnic path that we have found;
But yet compared to other days
And other times,
It seems a better route.
We lost our way before;
In fear,
And guilt,
Resentments held too long.
Self-pity had its way with us;
We found the perfect alibi
For all our faults.

We do not know what life may bring
From day to day.
Tomorrow is a task not yet begun,
And we could fail
To pass its test.
But this will wait,
While in Today we do the best
We can.
Today we try to grow.
Today we live,
We seek to know,
To give,
To share
With you.

Finis

TO THE READER

U. A. F. is an abbreviation for the Utah Alcoholism Foundation, a non-profit corporation dedicated to the furtherance of education, rehabilitation and research on alcoholism. The Foundation has no opinions or takes no stand on the wet or dry question.

The author of this book, Lewis F. Presnall, became identified with the Foundation through a previous writing "The Wife of the Alcoholic—A Pattern to Happiness." The publication gained wide acceptance not only by wives of alcoholics, but others confronted with the problems of life. Thousands of unsolicited letters of appreciation for the book have been received from individuals throughout the United States, Canada and other countries. This acceptance led to Mr. Presnall writing "Search for Serenity." We feel the book will prove enlightening and helpful to anyone seeking peace of mind in a troubled world of tensions and pressures.

In acknowledgment of request made by the author, should a profit be realized from the sale of this book, all funds so derived will be dedicated to the University of Utah School of Alcohol Studies.

Utah Alcoholism Foundation
2880 South Main
Suite 210
Salt Lake City, Utah 84115